KITCHEN CHEMISTRY

Science Experiments to Do at Home
KITCHEN CHEMISTRY

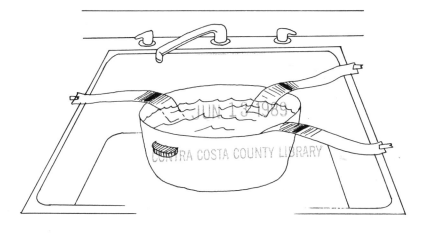

ROBERT GARDNER

Illustrated with photographs
and line drawings

JULIAN MESSNER

To Lisa, Joshua, Bryn, and Jennifer

JULIAN MESSNER and colophon are trademarks of
Simon & Schuster, Inc.   Design by Carol Fazio Kuchta.
Manufactured in the United States of America.

(Lib. ed.) 10 9 8 7 6 5 4 3 2 1

(Paper ed.) 10 9 8 7 6 5 4 3 2 1

Library of Congress Cataloging-in-Publication Data

Gardner, Robert, 1929–
  Kitchen chemistry.

  Includes index.
  1. Chemistry—Experiments—Juvenile literature.
I. Title.
QD38.G37   1989   542   88–23128
ISBN 0-671-67776-4
ISBN 0–671–67576–1 (pbk.)

Contents

Preface

Your kitchen, in addition to being a place to prepare meals and wash dishes, is a well-equipped science laboratory. You can heat materials on the stove, cool them in the refrigerator, and submerge objects in the sink. Hot and cold water is at your fingertips; ice cubes are but a step away; the oven will keep things at a constant warm temperature while the refrigerator and freezer can maintain constant cold temperatures. A young science enthusiast has more counter space in the family kitchen than most college students can find in their laboratories. Kitchen cabinets, pantries, and refrigerators are well stocked with the chemicals and other materials needed to perform a variety of interesting experiments.

This book describes experiments you can do at the kitchen counter, stove, sink, or refrigerator; a few require you to move all about the kitchen. Some of these experiments take time. You may have to leave your materials for several hours or days to see what happens. Be sure to leave lengthy experiments where they do not get in the way of people who have chores to do in the kitchen. Your parents will be happier about your experimentation if you don't interfere with their work and if you clean up after you finish each experiment. Thoughtful scientists do not allow their experimentation to keep others from their work. You should form the habit of working with care, especially in experiments that involve the stove or glass materials.

Science in the kitchen sometimes involves using things that can be dangerous, such as flames, matches, and chemicals that are poisonous. As you do the activities and experiments described in this or any other book, do them safely. Keep in mind the rules listed below and follow them faithfully.

1. Any experiments that you do should be done under the supervision of a parent, teacher, or another knowledgeable adult.

2. Read all instructions carefully. If you have questions, check with an adult. Don't take chances.

3. If you work with a friend who enjoys science too, maintain a serious attitude while experimenting. Horseplay can be dangerous to you and to others.

4. Do not taste chemicals unless instructed to do so. Many of them are poisonous.

5. Keep flammable materials such as alcohol away from flames and other sources of heat.

6. If you are using matches or flames, have a fire extinguisher nearby and know how to use it.

7. Keep the area where you are experimenting clean and organized. When you have finished, clean up and put away the materials you were using.

8. Don't touch glass that has just been heated. If you should get burned, rinse the area with cold water and apply ice.

9. Never experiment with the electricity that comes from wall outlets unless under the close supervision of a knowledgeable adult.

You can add to the value of the experiments you do by keeping notes on them. Set up an experiment notebook and record carefully the work you do and details like amounts and time involved. In doing some of these experiments, you may discover new questions that you can answer with experiments of your own. By all means, carry out these experiments (with your parents' or teacher's permission). You are developing the kind of curiosity that is shared by all scientists.

1

CHEMISTRY IN AND NEAR THE KITCHEN SINK

The most commonly used liquid in chemistry is water. It has very interesting properties of its own, and it provides a way of bringing chemicals together. What could be a more convenient place to investigate this common yet vital liquid than your own kitchen sink?

1. HEAPING LIQUIDS

You've seen baskets with berries, apples, or other fruit heaped well above the baskets' rims. Did you know that liquids can be heaped this way too?

Fill a medicine cup, test tube, or a vial (like the small vessels that pills from a drugstore come in) level to the brim with water. Use a medicine dropper to add more water to the container. You'll be amazed at how high you can heap water above the rim of the cup, tube, or vial. Use a ruler to estimate the height of the water. A piece of dark paper behind the heaped water will help you to see it better.

Your results should convince you that water holds together very well. It really sticks to itself.

Repeat the experiment, but this time count the number of drops of water you add to the brim-filled container before the water spills over the side. By counting the number of drops it takes to collect a fluid ounce or 10 milliliters of water, you can figure out what volume of water you heaped above the top.

Try adding straight pins to a glass filled to the brim with water. How many pins can you add to the glass before the water spills over the rim?

Do other liquids stick together as well as water? You can find out by heaping other liquids in the same or identical containers. Try measuring the heaped heights and volumes of such liquids as soapy water, alcohol, and cooking oil. If you use the same medicine dropper for all the liquids, be sure to clean and rinse it thoroughly between experiments.

Which liquid seems to stick together best?

A PREDICTION: Try to tell ahead of time what will happen if you add a drop of soapy water to plain water heaped well above the rim of a container. Try it. Were you right?

2. DROPS OF LIQUID ON WAXED PAPER

From the way different liquids heap, perhaps you can predict which liquid will form the biggest drops. It's difficult to measure the size of a single drop, but with a medicine cup and eyedropper, you can measure the volume of many drops and then divide to find the volume of just one drop.

Count the number of drops of water as you fill a medicine cup to the 10-ml line (10 ml or 10cc). If it takes 200 drops, then each drop is $\frac{1}{20}$ ml (10 ml/200 = $\frac{1}{20}$ ml).

Repeat the experiment using alcohol, soapy water, and cooking oil. Which liquid forms the largest drops?

After thoroughly cleaning and rinsing the medicine dropper, place a drop of plain water on a sheet of waxed paper. Look at the drop from the side. What does it look like? To see how water drops attract one another, place a second drop very close to the first one. You'll see the drops "leap" together.

Drop some small puddles of water on the waxed paper. Make two-drop, three-drop, five-drop, ten-drop, and twenty-drop puddles. How do these puddles compare in shape with the single-drop puddle?

Next, prepare similar puddles using soapy water. How do these drops and puddles compare with the plain water drops and puddles?

After thoroughly washing and rinsing the eyedropper, repeat the experiment again using drops of alcohol.

Then try drops of cooking oil. How do these drops and puddles compare with those made from plain and soapy water?

3. DROPS OF LIQUID ON DIFFERENT SURFACES

Does the surface on which you place a drop affect its shape? To find out, place a drop of water on waxed paper, aluminum foil, plastic wrap, glass, and newspaper. Look at these drops from the side. Does the surface the water drops are on affect their shape?

Repeat the experiment using drops of alcohol, soapy water, and cooking oil. Does the surface affect the shape of these drops?

A PREDICTION: A liquid drop on a surface has a shape like the lens in a magnifying glass or microscope. Can you predict which liquid—water, alcohol, soapy water, or cooking oil—will magnify the most? To test your prediction, place a drop of each liquid over identical letters on some newspaper print. Which liquid makes the letter look biggest? If the liquid sinks into the paper, place a sheet of clear plastic wrap or waxed paper over the print.

Was your prediction correct?

4. CLIMBING WATER

The force of gravity pulls everything toward the center of the earth. That's why a stone or ball falls to the ground when you release it; it's why you always come back down no matter how high you jump. But in this experiment you'll discover forces stronger than gravity—forces that cause water and other liquids to climb upward, defying the force of gravity.

To see water defy gravity, cut a one-inch-wide strip from a paper towel. Hang the paper strip so that one end is in some water as shown in Figure 1. Add a few drops of food coloring or ink to the water so you can watch the water move into the paper. (You may find the dyes in the coloring or ink separating into different colors as water rises in the paper.)

Where is the liquid level in the paper strip after several hours? How high will it be tomorrow? Will it continue to rise forever?

You might like to see how water rises in other materials. You could try other brands of paper towels, different kinds of cloth, blotter paper, string, wood, and other substances.

Does water rise to different levels in different materials?

Repeat this experiment using a paper towel strip that is covered with a tube made from waxed paper. You can seal the edges of the waxed paper with tape. (See Figure 2.) Can you explain why the water rises higher in the covered strip than it did in the one that was uncovered? If not, try the next experiment.

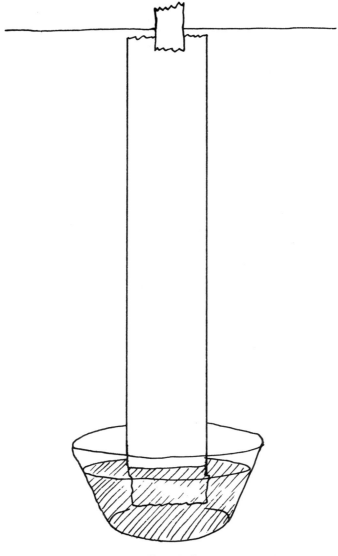

Figure 1

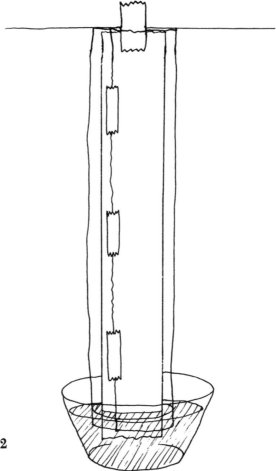

Figure 2

5. DRYING WET TOWELS

Wet two identical paper towels. Hang one in the air. Put the other towel in a covered container. Which towel dries faster? Can you now explain why water rose higher when the paper towel strip was covered?

But the basic question is still unanswered: How can water defy gravity in the paper strips you have tested?

6. How Water Defies Gravity

To understand how water rises in a paper towel, you first need to see what a paper towel or blotter is made of. Tear apart a small piece of paper towel. Look at the edges of the torn paper through a magnifying glass or a microscope. You will see that the towel is made up of tiny wood fibers packed very close together. Under a good microscope, you can see water rising in the tiny spaces *between* the fibers when the towel's edge is dipped in water.

The rise of water in narrow spaces is called *capillarity*. But giving it a name doesn't mean we understand it. We do know that water is a very *cohesive* liquid: it sticks together well. That is why water can form such large drops. Water also adheres (sticks) to many other materials. If you turn a wet dish over, some of the water will remain stuck to the dish. The adhesion between water and glass and water and many other materials shows us that there are strong attractive forces between water and these materials.

The force of attraction between water and wood or cloth fibers causes water to move into the tiny spaces between these fibers. Because water itself is very cohesive, the water adhering to the fibers is in contact with

17

portions of water not touching the fibers. This water is pulled upward by the cohesive forces between it and water that has adhered to the wood fibers.

You can see how water adheres to glass and how it rises higher as the spaces grow smaller by doing the following experiment. Place two clean, dry water glasses in a tray of colored water. Move the sides of the two glasses very close together and watch the water rise in the small space between the two glasses. What happens to the water level as you move the glasses closer together? Farther apart?

You can use two flat pieces of glass such as windowpanes to illustrate this effect even more clearly. (**Be careful not to cut your hands!**) Bind the glass plates together with a pair of large rubber bands. Place a thin strip of

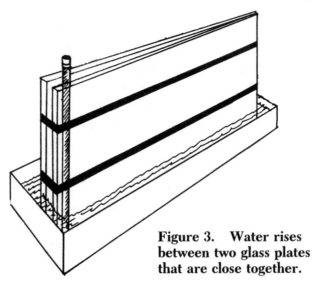

Figure 3. Water rises between two glass plates that are close together.

wood or plastic between the plates at one end to form a thin wedge of air. Put the glass plates in a tray of colored water and watch the water rise between the plates. (See Figure 3.) See if you can predict at which end of the air wedge the water will rise higher.

Look closely at the surface of the water in a vial. Notice that the water level is highest where the water touches the glass. The curved surface of the water is called the *meniscus* (mi nis' kes). From what you have found in these experiments, can you explain why water has a meniscus?

Using Capillarity to Color Flowers

During the summer you can probably find Queen Anne's Lace blooming in a field near your home. Cut a few such flowers and bring them into your kitchen. Put one or two stalks in several small glasses of water. Add a different food coloring to the water in each glass.

Watch the white petals of these flowers over several hours. Do the food colors ascend the stalks of these flowers the way they do strips of paper towel? How can you tell?

Can you produce new colors by mixing the food colors that you add to the water in the glasses?

Carefully split the stem of a Queen Anne's Lace, a white carnation, or any white flower. Place one side of the stem in water colored with red food coloring and the other in water colored by green or blue food coloring.

Will you obtain a two-colored flower? Or will the colors mix to produce a third color?

7. MORE EXPERIMENTS WITH CLIMBING LIQUIDS

Will other liquids climb paper towels as well as water, or are they less defiant of gravity?

To find out, place the lower ends of identical hanging strips of paper towel in soapy water, alcohol, cooking oil, salt water, and plain water. Leave the strips for several days. What do you find? Are the results different if the strips are covered with waxed paper? Does the width of the paper towel strip affect the height to which the water rises?

Try strips of different widths in colored water. Make some as narrow as one-fourth inch; others could be one-half inch, one, two, and three inches wide. How do you explain the results?

You can make a paper-towel siphon. Just place one end of a folded paper towel in a tray of water on your kitchen counter. Let the other end of the towel hang into the sink. The towel acts like a siphon and transfers water from the tray to the sink.

Will the siphon work if you raise the end that is in the sink until it is higher than the water level in the tray?

8. SEPARATING COLORS

Chemists sometimes separate chemicals by a method known as *chromatography*. To see how chromatography works, cut several one-inch-wide strips from a paper towel or, better, from a sheet of white blotter paper. Using a watercolor paint-brush or a toothpick, paint a stripe of red food coloring across one of the strips about two inches from one end. When the food coloring is dry, suspend the tip of the paper strip nearest the colored stripe in a container of water in the sink. Tape the other end to the side of the sink. (Figure 4.)

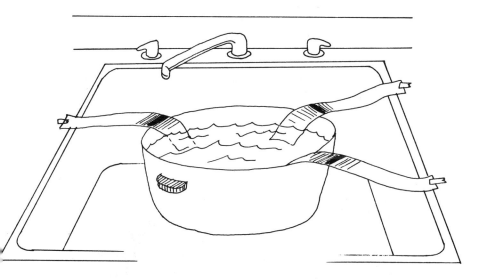

Figure 4. Chromatography in the sink.

Watch what happens as water carries the food coloring along the paper strip. Did the food coloring contain more than one dye? How can you tell?

Repeat the experiment using fresh strips. Paint stripes of different food coloring, black ink, Mercurochrome, and mixtures of food colorings, and ink and Mercurochrome. What do you find?

9. WHICH PAPER TOWEL IS BEST?

You can find many different brands of paper towels in a supermarket and see the commercials for them on television. Which brand is best?

The answer to that question depends on how you want to use the towel and how much money it's worth to you. But you can certainly test to see which towel absorbs the most water, which one absorbs water fastest, and which one is strongest.

Test 1: How Much Water Does Each Brand of Towel Absorb?

To find out, pour 8 ounces (230 ml) of water into a measuring cup. Take two paper towels of the same brand; fold and submerge them in the cup. When the towels are thoroughly wet, remove them from the water and let any excess water drip back into the cup. How much water is left in the cup? How much water did the towels absorb? Repeat this experiment for each brand of towel. Which brand absorbs the most water per towel?

How many towels are in each roll of each different brand? Which brand absorbs the most water per roll?

How much did each roll cost? Which brand is the best buy in terms of water absorbed per penny?

Test 2: Which Towel Absorbs Water Fastest?

Fold two paper towels from a roll and dip one end into 8 ounces (230 ml) of water in a measuring cup. As water flows into the towel, keep the water level in the towel even with the water level in the cup. After one minute, remove the towel and let the excess water drip back into the cup. How much water did the towels absorb in one minute?

Repeat this test for each brand of towel. Which brand absorbs water fastest?

Test 3: Which Towel Is Strongest?

Place a large plastic bowl or dish at the center of a *dry* paper towel. (See the photo on page 24.) Have a friend hold the towel over the sink while you add measured amounts of water to the plastic bowl. Be careful not to wet the towel. How many ounces (milliliters) of water can the towel support before it breaks?

Repeat the experiment using different brands. Which brand of towel is strongest when dry?

"Do you think it'll hold another cup?"

24

How can you find out which brand of towel is strongest when wet?

10. FALLING WATER

When a thin stream of water falls from a faucet, it breaks into drops. Does the size of the stream affect the point at which the water pulls itself together to form drops? You can find out by punching two holes in the bottom of a Styrofoam cup. Use a pin to punch a hole about 1/16 inch (1.5 mm) in diameter in one side of the bottom of the cup. Use a small nail to punch a hole twice as wide about an inch from the smaller hole. Punch the holes from the *inside out* so you can pull away any pieces of Styrofoam around the holes that might make the streams irregular. (See Figure 5.)

Fill the cup with water and compare the distances the two streams fall before they form drops. (See the

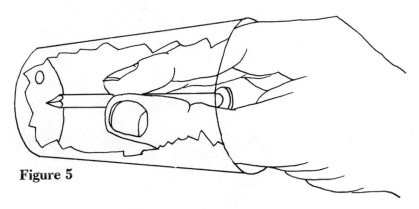

Figure 5

"Look! This stream is longer."

photo on page 26.) Use a ruler to measure the length of the unbroken columns.

Does the water level in the cup affect the length of the unbroken columns? Which stream stops flowing first? Why do you think the water stops flowing from both holes before the cup is completely empty?

Fill the cup with soapy water and measure the length of the unbroken liquid columns. Because streams of soapy water are very sensitive to vibrations or movements, it would be wise to rest the cup on the edge of a stool or chair over the sink. The soapy water can be collected in a container placed in the sink so that you can repeat your measurements. Why do you think the soapy-water streams are longer than the plain-water streams of the same diameter?

11. WATER'S SKIN

Water holds together so well that it behaves as if it had an invisible skin. To see this for yourself, fill a clean, well-rinsed container with water. Using a fork or a bent paper clip, gently place a paper clip, needle, or straight pin on the water's surface. Amazingly, the water surface will support the small piece of metal. Look closely! You will see that the water surface is "bent" much as the skin on your palm bends when you push it with your finger. (See the photo on page 28.)

Notice the dimples in water's skin.

What happens to the floating piece of metal if you add a single drop of liquid soap to the water?

Do you think the small piece of metal can be made to float on soapy water? On alcohol? On cooking oil?

12. DISAPPEARING SOLIDS

Have you ever watched colored, flavored crystals disappear in water as you stirred them while preparing a cool drink on a hot day? When a solid, such as sugar, disappears in a liquid, we say the solid, or *solute*, has dissolved in the liquid, or *solvent*, to make a *solution*.

Can you dissolve as much solid as you want in water, or is there a limit? Will solids dissolve in liquids other than water? Will liquids dissolve in other liquids? Will gases dissolve in liquids? Does temperature have any effect on the preparation of solutions? Can you dissolve two solutes in the same solvent? Can you separate solute from solvent once a solution is made? Will stirring make a solute dissolve faster?

The following experiments will enable you to answer these questions. Be sure to label and save the solutions you make so that you can use them again.

To Stir or Not to Stir?

Place a teaspoon of sugar in each of two glasses that contain the same amount of water. Use a spoon to stir the water and sugar in one glass but not the other.

Does stirring make sugar dissolve faster? Will stirring make salt dissolve faster?

Sugar in Water

Use a measuring cup to add 4 ounces (120 ml) of cold water to a clean drinking glass. Add a level teaspoon of sugar to the water. (You can use a card or ruler to sweep off crystals above the edge of the spoon.) Stir the water until all the sugar dissolves. How many teaspoons of sugar can you dissolve in the water? Can you taste the sugar in the water?

When no more solid can be dissolved in the solvent, we say the solution is *saturated.*

A PREDICTION: See if you can predict how many teaspoons of sugar you will need to make a saturated solution using 8 ounces (240 ml) of water. Were you right?

A Hot Solution

Repeat the experiment, but this time use 4 ounces (120 ml) of *hot* water. How much sugar does it take to make a saturated solution when you use hot water? Does the temperature of the water change the amount of sugar that can be dissolved in 4 ounces of water?

Pour the clear, hot solution into another glass to separate it from any dissolved sugar at the bottom of the first glass. Look at the clear, hot solution every few minutes as it cools. What happens? Taste the solid that collects at the bottom of the glass. What is it? Why do you think it comes out of solution?

Salt Solutions

How much salt (sodium chloride) will dissolve in 4 ounces (120 ml) of cold water? (Use kosher salt if possible. Most other table salts contain additives that may make the solution cloudy.) Can you taste the salt in the water?

Try to predict how much salt will dissolve in 8 ounces (240 ml) of cold water. Were you right?

Do you think more salt will dissolve in 8 ounces of hot water? Try it. Are you surprised by what you find?

13. OTHER DISAPPEARING SOLIDS

Are all solids soluble in water? Try these substances that can be found in most kitchens: baking soda (bicarbonate of soda), flour, starch, instant tea or coffee, and regular ground coffee. Add a teaspoon of each to separate glasses of water. Which solids disappear (dissolve) in water? A cloudy mixture that does not clear up with stirring means that tiny particles of the solid are spread through the water. They haven't really disappeared (dissolved). In a few minutes, they will settle to the bottom of the glass.

14. FILTERING

To separate undissolved solids from a solution, a chemist uses a filter. You can make your own filter by folding a paper towel and placing it in a funnel as shown in Figure 6.

Pour one of the salt or sugar solutions you prepared earlier through the filter paper in the funnel. Taste some

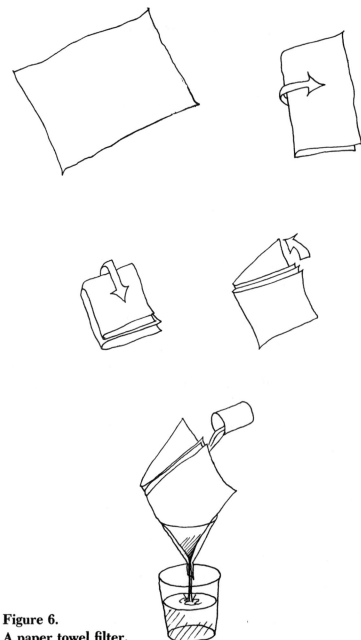

Figure 6.
A paper towel filter.

of the liquid that comes through the filter. Does the filter remove solids that are dissolved? How can you tell?

Pour a little of the liquid that came through the filter into a saucer. Place the saucer in a warm place for several days so that the liquid will evaporate. When the saucer is dry, what additional evidence do you have that the dissolved solid came through the filter?

What happens when you pour a mixture of flour and water or starch and water through a filter? Does the flour or starch mixture pass through the filter? Will undissolved sugar or salt go through the filter?

15. TWO SOLUTES IN ONE SOLVENT

Will sugar dissolve in a saturated solution of salt and water? Add a teaspoon of sugar to a glass half full of saturated salt solution. Does the sugar dissolve?

Do you think salt will dissolve in a saturated solution of sugar and water? Try it. Were you right?

16. OTHER SOLVENTS

Will salt, sugar, and baking soda dissolve in liquids other than water? Try dissolving each of the solids in soapy water, alcohol, cooking oil, and vinegar. Which solids are soluble in each liquid? What happened when you added baking soda to vinegar?

A PREDICTION: What volume do you expect to find if you add 2 fluid ounces (60 ml) of hot water to 2 fluid ounces of solid sugar? Try it. Were you right? How can you explain the results of this experiment?

If you measure out equal *weights* of sugar and water and then mix them to form a solution, what do you think the total weight of the solution will be? Were you right this time?

17. LIQUIDS IN LIQUIDS

When a liquid such as alcohol dissolves in water, we say the liquids are *miscible*. Add some cooking oil to half a glass of water. Are these liquids miscible? Stir the oil and water to break up the oil into tiny droplets. When the oil droplets are spread through the water, the mixture of liquids is called an emulsion. If you stop stirring, the oil droplets soon collect in a separate layer above the water.

To make a longer-lasting emulsion add a few drops of liquid detergent to the oil and water before you stir it again. Do you see why a detergent is used to remove insoluble materials from dirty clothes or dishes?

18. A KITCHEN PRINTER

With the aid of chemistry you can make copies of newspaper photographs in your own kitchen. To prepare a copying fluid, mix about 2 ounces (60 ml) of turpentine with 4 ounces (120 ml) of tap water. (**Turpentine is poisonous. Be sure to clean everything thoroughly after you finish this experiment.**) How many layers of liquid do you have? Which liquid is on top? If you had equal volumes of water and turpentine, which liquid do you think would be heavier?

If you stir the two liquids together, will they stay mixed? What happens when you stop stirring?

Add about 20 to 30 drops of liquid detergent or a small piece of soap to the mixture and stir again. This time you'll see a cloudy mixture because the soap or detergent allows an emulsion to form.

To make a copy, first find a good newspaper photograph. Place the photo on some old newspapers on your kitchen counter. Use a small paint brush to spread the emulsion you have made over the photo. Then lay a sheet of white paper over the wet picture. Rub the white paper all over with the bottom of a soup spoon. The turpentine will dissolve some of the print in the picture. Rubbing the photo and white paper together will transfer the dissolved ink onto the blank paper.

Carefully remove the paper and look at your copy. How does it compare with the original? Do you have an exact copy or a mirror image of the original?

19. Do Gases Dissolve in Liquids?

The next time you open a bottle of soda, watch closely. What do you see that makes you believe there is a gas dissolved in the liquid? From this observation what can you tell about the effect of pressure on the solubility of a gas in a liquid? Try warming an open bottle of soda by placing it in a pan of hot water. How does temperature affect the solubility of a gas in a liquid? Pour some very cold water into a glass. Place the glass in a warm place and look at the liquid again after several hours. Notice the bubbles that collect in the water. These are bubbles of air that were dissolved in the water when it was colder. Is air more soluble in hot or cold water?

20. DO GASES DISSOLVE IN OTHER GASES?

Your television or radio weather forecaster often talks about humidity. High humidity means that a lot of water vapor is dissolved in air. To see that water is dissolved in air, half fill a shiny metal can with warm water. Add small pieces of ice to the water and stir. Continue to add ice until a fine film of water begins to form on the cold can. This water, or dew, was dissolved in the air. As the air in contact with the can cools, the solution of water in air becomes saturated. As it cools further, the extra water that can't dissolve condenses on the cold can.

A PREDICTION: The water that comes from the faucets in your kitchen is under pressure. If you nearly fill a clear quart or liter soda bottle with cold water, what do you expect to see rising to the top of the liquid? Were you right?

If you repeat the experiment using hot water, what will be different?

21. GENIE IN A BOTTLE

You've heard that hot air rises. Does hot water rise too?

Look at the photo on page 38 of the two bottles. A dark, wispy genie seems to be emerging from the lower bottle and rising into the upper one. To find out where the genie comes from, you can do this experiment yourself.

Find two bottles with narrow necks (soft drink bottles work well). Completely fill one bottle with hot water and enough black ink to make the liquid look very dark. Fill the second bottle with cold water. Place a small piece of paper towel over the opening of the bottle that contains cold, clear water. Then carefully turn that bottle upside down and place it on top of the bottle that contains the inky water. Why doesn't the water run out when you tip the bottle upside down?

Carefully pull the piece of paper from between the two bottles and watch the genie rise.

To see why the genie rises, fill an eyedropper with some warm water that has been colored with ink or food coloring. Place the tip of the eyedropper in some cold water as shown in Figure 7. *Slowly* squeeze some of the colored, warm water into the clear, cold water.

Does the warm water rise or sink in the cold water?

A genie rises
from the
bottle.

Figure 7

Try this experiment again, but this time squeeze a little colored, cold water into some clear, warm water. Does the cold liquid rise or fall in the warm water?

Would the genie rise if you used cold water in the lower bottle and hot water in the upper bottle? Try it and see.

Using food coloring and hot and cold water, see if you can prepare different colored genies. Can you make a red genie? A green one? How about a blue one?

22. FIRE EXTINGUISHER GAS

You can produce the gas found in fire extinguishers by adding vinegar to baking soda. But first, place a birthday candle in a small piece of clay for support. (**Ask a parent or another adult to help you with this experiment.**) Then cover the bottom of a wide-mouth jar (a clean, empty, peanut butter jar works well) with baking soda. Slowly pour an ounce of vinegar over the baking soda. The frothy bubbles that form are filled with carbon dioxide. Because this gas is heavier than an equal volume of air, it will soon force all the air out of the jar.

Light the candle. (**Be careful lighting matches.**) Hold the jar above the candle and tip it so as to pour the gas (not the liquid) onto the flame. You will see the flame go out as the carbon dioxide falls over it forcing air away from the candle.

In a carbon dioxide fire extinguisher this gas is stored in a cylinder under high pressure. When the nozzle is opened, the gas rushes out and cools as it expands. The heavy gas covers and smothers a fire.

23. SINKING BUBBLES, FLOATING BUBBLES

If you don't have a bubble-making kit, buy one in

a toy department. It's a bargain! After you've had some fun making air-filled bubbles and watching the beautiful colors that form, you can have some more fun making carbon dioxide bubbles. Figure 8 shows how you can do this by dipping the wide end of an eyedropper connected to a carbon dioxide generator into a dish of bubble-making liquid. Let the bubble fill with carbon dioxide gas and then gently shake the bubble off the eyedropper.

You can make carbon dioxide by dropping Alka-Seltzer® tablets into water or by adding vinegar to baking soda.

Do bubbles of carbon dioxide fall faster than air-filled bubbles of the same size?

You can make air-filled bubbles float or even rise if you let them fall into a pail or sink filled with carbon

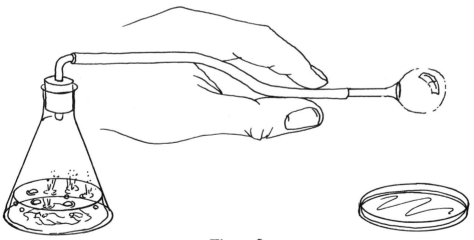

Figure 8

dioxide. To see this, cover the bottom of a pail or sink with a thin coat of baking soda. Then add half a pint of vinegar to the powder. (Add a pint of vinegar if you use a sink.)

Let some air-filled bubbles fall into the carbon dioxide-filled pail or sink. Why do the bubbles float above the pail or sink?

24. SINKING BALLOONS, FLOATING BALLOONS

Just as air-filled bubbles will float on an atmosphere of carbon dioxide, so alcohol-filled balloons will float in water. Use a measuring cup, a funnel, or a small beaker to fill a balloon with rubbing alcohol. Seal the neck of the balloon shut with a tie band, being careful not to let any air into the balloon.

Place your alcohol-balloon "boat" in a pail or deep pan of cold water. Test the cargo-carrying capacity of your boat by seeing how many paper clips or washers you can hang on the tie band before the boat sinks.

Empty the balloon and fill it with hot water. What is the cargo carrying capacity of this boat?

A balloon with cold water will sink in hot water, but here's a way to raise the sunken ship and turn it into a submarine. Drop a balloon filled with cold water into a jar three-fourths full of hot water. Carefully and slowly add some saturated salt solution down the side

42

of the jar. The balloon will rise and come to rest like a stalled submarine beneath the surface.

To see why the sunken ship rises, color some saturated salt solution with food coloring. Where does this colored solution go when you pour it slowly down the side of a jar of water? Which is heavier, equal volumes of a salt solution or warm water? Alcohol or water? Hot water or cold water?

25. A Boat with Power

The boats you made in Experiment 24 didn't move. To make a jet-powered boat, cut one long side from a half-gallon milk carton. The narrow top of the carton is the bow of your boat. Cut a small hole near the center of the bottom of the carton. (See Figure 9.)

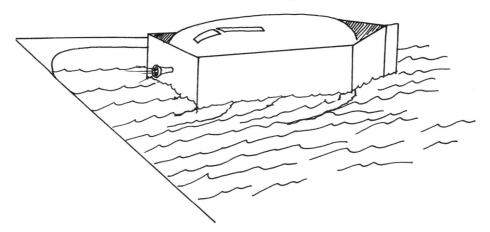

Figure 9.   A jet-powered boat

The jet power can come from a hot-dog shaped balloon. Run the neck of the balloon through the hole in the bottom of the carton. Blow up the balloon, and as you let go of the neck of the balloon your lung air will provide the power needed to move the boat across the sink or bathtub sea.

26. BENDING WATER

Look at the water stream in the photo on page 45. It's being bent by a rubber rod that was rubbed on some woolen clothing. You can get similar results by rubbing a plastic comb or ruler on your clothes or on a paper towel and then holding the comb or ruler near a thin stream of water flowing from your kitchen faucet. Unless it's a humid summer day, the stream will bend toward the "magic wand."

When you rubbed the plastic, it became electrically charged. We believe there are charges in the smallest particles of water, too. We call these tiny particles *molecules*. The electrical charges are not spread evenly over a water molecule. One end is slightly negative; the other end has a small positive charge. If a plastic ruler has a positive charge, it will attract the negative ends of the water molecules and pull them toward the plastic. The positive ends of the molecules are repelled by the plastic and will turn so that the negative ends of the molecules are closer to the positively charged plastic.

What will happen if the plastic is negatively charged?

A stream of water near an electrically charged rod

2

CHEMISTRY IN THE REFRIGERATOR

Much of chemistry involves what happens when substances change from liquids to solids, or when their temperatures drop dramatically. A refrigerator enables the kitchen chemist to study such changes.

1. COOLING A GAS

What happens to a gas as it cools? To find out, you can experiment with a gas that is free and plentiful—air.

Attach a balloon to the neck of each of two empty 1-quart soft drink bottles. The balloons should be inflated only enough to make them stand up; don't blow up the balloons so that they are stretched.

Put one bottle in a cold place such as a freezer. Leave the other bottle in a warm room. After an hour or so, remove the bottle from the freezer and compare

46

the two. Which one has the bigger volume of air now? What happens to the volume of air when it cools in a closed container?

Leave both bottles in the same room for a while. What happens to the volume of the cold gas as it warms?

Do other gases behave in the same way when they cool? You can find out by placing an ounce (30 ml) of vinegar in each of the two bottles. Then put a teaspoonful of baking soda on each of two small pieces of paper. Fold the papers over the white solid to make two small packets. Drop one packet into each of the two quart bottles. When the reaction in a bottle is nearly complete, pull the mouth of a balloon over the neck of the bottle. What gas is in these bottles?

Put the bottles in cold and warm places as before. What happens to the volume of the carbon dioxide as it cools?

By carefully measuring the volume changes as a gas cools or warms, you would find that *all* gases expand or shrink by $\frac{1}{273}$ of their volume for each degree Celsius temperature change above or below 0°C, or $\frac{1}{494}$ of their volume for each Fahrenheit-degree change above or below 32°F.

2. MELTING ICE

The freezer compartment of your refrigerator is a good place to prepare the ice and ice cubes you will need to carry out the experiments that will enable you to answer a number of questions about melting and freezing ice.

Will an Ice Cube Melt Faster in Air or in Water?

The answer could depend on the temperature of the air and water. You might guess that ice will melt faster in hot water than in cold air. Let's refine the question. Will an ice cube melt faster in air or in water if both the air and water are at the *same* temperature?

With a thermometer you can find the temperature of the air in your kitchen. By mixing hot and cold water, you can make the water temperature in a dishpan equal to the temperature of the air. When you have succeeded in doing this, place one ice cube in the water. At the same time, place an identical ice cube on a folded paper towel on the kitchen counter. Where does the ice melt faster?

Here's another experiment that will help you answer this question. Place an ice cube in some shallow water so that about half of the ice is in water and half is in air. Watch to see how the ice cube melts. What can you conclude from this experiment?

Will the Amount of Water Affect an Ice Cube's Melting Speed?

Fill identical containers with different volumes of water at the same temperature. You might use one-half cup, one cup, two cups, and four cups of water. Add identical ice cubes to each volume of water. Does the amount of water affect the time it takes an ice cube to melt?

In which container does the water become coldest? How can you explain this?

Does the Temperature of the Water in Which the Ice Melts Affect the Ice Cube's Melting Speed?

Because you want to test the effect of temperature (not volume of water) on melting speed, you should use equal amounts of water in identical containers. You might have the water in one container at 40°F (5°C), another at 60°F (16°C), another at 80°F (27°C), and so on.

If you used different volumes of water and different containers, you would not know whether it was the different temperatures, or the different volumes, or the different containers that affected the melting speed. By using equal volumes of water and identical containers, you can be sure that any differences in the melting times of the identical ice cubes that you drop into these containers will be caused by the different temperatures. A good experiment should test the effect of only one thing at a time.

How does the temperature of the water around the ice affect the melting speed? Does doubling the temperature double the speed?

Does Stirring Affect the Melting Speed of an Ice Cube?

Design an experiment to answer this question. How many containers do you need? How should the temperature and volume of water in each container compare?

Will Crushing the Ice Affect Its Melting Speed?

You can crush an ice cube by placing it in a plastic bag and tapping it with a hammer. Place the bag in a container and use the bag to line the container. Pour a pint or quart of water into the plastic-lined container and see how long it takes for the crushed ice to melt.

Pour out the water and repeat the experiment, but use an ice cube that has not been crushed. How much water should you use this time? What should its temperature be?

What do your results indicate about the effect of crushing the ice? Why do you think crushing ice affects its melting speed? The next experiment may help you to answer this question.

Does the Amount of Surface that Ice Has Affect Its Melting Speed?

The surface (the outside) of an ice cube or anything else has an area. You could measure the area of an ice cube by seeing how many one-inch or one-centimeter squares you could fit on the surface of the ice. To find out if surface area affects melting speed, you can make two pieces of ice, each with a different surface area but the same volume.

To make a piece of ice with a large surface area, pour an ounce (about 30 ml) of water into a wide, shallow container such as a plastic lid, cover, or plate. You can use one section in an ice cube tray or an individual ice cube container to make a piece of ice with the same volume but a much smaller surface. When both pieces of ice are thoroughly frozen, put them in a pan or pail of water. Which piece melts faster? In which piece was more ice touching warm water?

Does the Shape of an Ice Cube Affect Its Melting Speed?

Try to figure out a way to make a cone-shaped piece of ice. How about a sphere (ball)? A cylinder?

Prepare these shapes, a regular ice cube, and a flat, pancake-shaped one like the one you made in the last experiment. Use the same amount of water to make each of the shapes. Which shape do you think will melt fastest? Slowest?

Place all the frozen shapes in a dishpan full of water. Was your prediction right? Which shape do you think had the largest surface area? Which one had the smallest surface area?

How Cold Can You Make Water by Adding Ice or Snow?

Place enough water in a glass or plastic container to cover the bulb of a thermometer. What is the temperature of the water? Add about an ounce (30 ml) of snow (it, too, is frozen water) or crushed ice and stir the ice and water mixture. What is the temperature now? Continue adding snow or crushed ice. How low does the temperature drop? Why do you think the temperature reaches a point below which it will not fall no matter how much ice or snow you add to the water?

How Cold Can You Make Water if You Put It in a Freezer?

Use a thermometer to find the temperature inside a freezer. Then place in the freezer a small container of water with a thermometer in it. The thermometer bulb should be under water as shown in Figure 10.

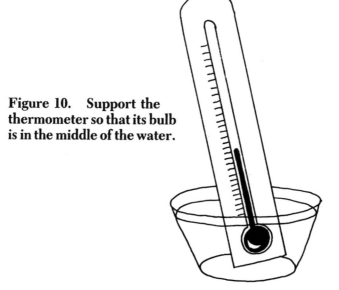

Figure 10.   Support the thermometer so that its bulb is in the middle of the water.

You may find it helpful to place the container near one side of the freezer so that the freezer wall can support the thermometer. Record the temperature of the water when you begin the experiment and every five or ten minutes thereafter until the temperature will fall no further.

Make a graph of your readings like the one in Figure 11. What is the temperature of the water while it is freezing? How does the temperature of freezing water

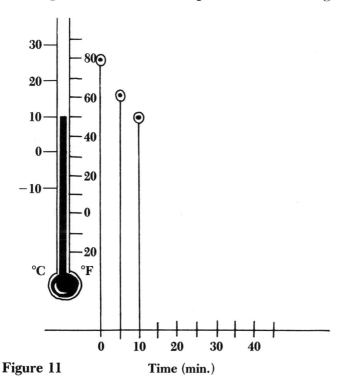

Figure 11   **Time (min.)**

compare with the temperature of the ice and water mixture you examined in the previous experiment?

How cold does the ice get after it has frozen? How does the final lowest temperature of the ice compare with the temperature of the freezer which you measured at the beginning of this experiment?

How Warm Does Ice Get Before It Melts?

In the last experiment you probably found that water freezes at about 32°F (0°C). In fact, that's how manufacturers know where to mark 32°F or 0°C on a thermometer scale.

At what temperature do you think ice will melt?

Test your prediction by removing from the freezer the container of ice with the thermometer in it that you made in the last experiment. Record the temperature of the ice as you begin and at five minute intervals thereafter until the thermometer bulb is no longer imbedded in ice. At what temperature does ice melt? How does this temperature compare with the freezing temperature of water?

Can You Make the Temperature of Melting Ice Lower than 32°F (0°C)?

Make a mixture of water and lots of crushed ice or snow. What's the temperature of this mix? Add one-fourth cup of salt to the ice and water mixture and stir.

What's the temperature now? What happens to the temperature as you add more salt? How low can you make the temperature by adding more salt?

Now you can understand why people often put salt on icy roads or walks. What does the salt do to the freezing temperatures? Will other substances lower the freezing temperature? How about sugar? Sand? Milk? Vinegar?

Can You Lift an Ice Cube Without Touching It?

To lift an ice cube from a glass of water without touching the ice, simply lay a short piece of thin string or thread on top of the ice cube. Then sprinkle some salt from a salt shaker on the ice around the string. After a minute or two, you will be able to lift the ice cube out of the water with the string. The string will be stuck to the ice.

To see how this works, watch closely when the salt is added. The salt causes the ice around the string to melt. However, a mixture of salt and water freezes at a temperature below 32°F (0°C). The low temperature causes some of the less salty water around the string to freeze so that it becomes stuck to the ice.

3. MAKING ICE CREAM

You may know that homemade ice cream can be prepared using a mixture of salt and ice to freeze a mixture of sugar and cream. You will need to use an ice cream maker. With the old-fashioned kind of ice cream maker a crank must be turned to mix the cream and sugar, but the result is well worth the work required.

To make vanilla ice cream heat a cup of cream over low heat. (**Have an adult help you.**) Be sure the cream does not boil. Stir about 1 cup of sugar and ⅛ teaspoon of salt into the cream until all the solid dissolves.

Allow this mixture to cool. Then add 3 more cups of cream and 1½ teaspoons of vanilla. Chill the mixture in a refrigerator.

When the creamy mixture is chilled, pour it into the container of the ice cream maker. Pack the freezing part of the ice cream maker about one-third full of chipped ice. Then add rock salt. The ratio of salt to ice should be about one to three. Continue to add ice and salt in the same ratio until the freezer is full.

Turn the cream slowly at first. When you begin to feel some resistance, turn faster. Continue turning (you may want some one to relieve you) until the creamy mixture is very stiff.

Pour off the salt water, and distribute the ice cream. If you want to keep the ice cream to use as a dessert, spoon it from the mixer into a plastic container that you can place in the freezing compartment of your refrigerator.

If you continue to make ice cream, you may want to prepare different flavors using chocolate chips, fresh fruits, and various sauces. You can find ice cream recipes in many cook books.

4. Sinking Ice, Floating Ice

Place an ice cube in a glass of water. Why do you think it floats?

If you think it's because of the tiny air bubbles in the ice, try this. Chip off a small piece of ice that has no air bubbles, or buy some clear, bubbleless ice cubes. You will find that clear ice floats in water too.

Giant drops of water form when ice melts in cooking oil.

Now add an ice cube to half a glass of alcohol. Why do you think the ice sinks?

An ice cube will float in cooking oil, but just barely. It's beautiful to see because the melting ice forms giant drops of water that fall ever so slowly through the clear, thick oil. It's like watching rain drops falling in slow motion.

Perhaps ice is heavier than alcohol but lighter than water and cooking oil, but before testing this idea, we'd better decide what "heaviness" means. Certainly, an ice cube weighs more than a drop of water, and the weight of a pint of alcohol exceeds the weight of a thimbleful of water. When people say oil is lighter than water, they usually mean that a certain volume of oil weighs less than an equal volume of water. If a cup of water weighs one-half pound, they would predict that a cup of oil would weigh less than one-half pound.

You can test this idea by comparing the weights of equal volumes of water, alcohol, cooking oil, and ice. If you don't have a balance or scale, you can make a fairly sensitive balance with a yardstick, some nails, string, and plastic or paper plates, as shown in Figure 12.

You can make a support for the fulcrum nail (the one at the 18-inch line) from wood, or you can simply let the ends of the nail rest on a pair of tall cans.

You'll need two small identical containers, such as vials or plastic medicine cups, to measure out equal volumes of ice, water, alcohol, and cooking oil. If the

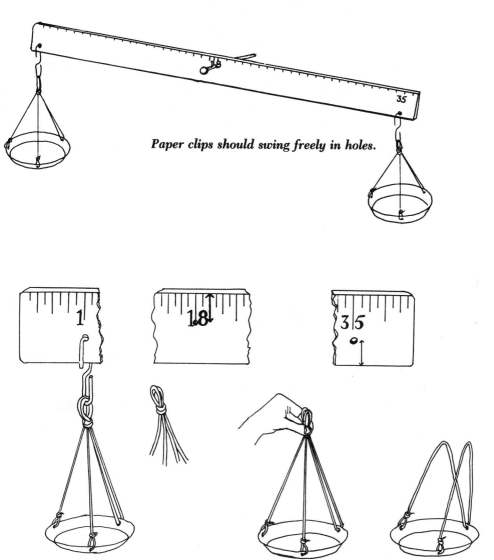

Paper clips should swing freely in holes.

Figure 12.   Make your own balance.

two containers don't have quite the same weight, you can make their weights equal by taping paper or paper clips to the lighter one.

Pour water into one container until it is about three-quarters full. Mark the water level with a marking pen or a piece of tape before you put the container into the freezer.

When the water is thoroughly frozen, remove it from the freezer and note where the top of the ice is compared with the original water level. What happened to the volume as the water froze?

Place the second container next to the container of ice. Add water to the empty container until you have equal volumes of ice and water. Put the two containers on the pans at opposite ends of the balance. Which is heavier, ice or water?

In the same way, compare equal volumes of ice and alcohol, alcohol and water, and water and cooking oil. Which substance is the heaviest? Which is lightest?

Do your measurements of heaviness for the same volume help you to explain why ice floats in water but sinks in alcohol?

What do you predict will happen if your pour cooking oil into alcohol? Try it. Were you right?

5. Keeping Ice

It's easy to keep ice in a freezer where the temperature is below 32°F (0°C), but how did people keep ice before electric or gas freezers were invented? Even during the first third of this century, many people had iceboxes. An iceman would deliver a large cake of ice weighing 20 to 100 pounds and place it in an insulated icebox. People stored food in the icebox just as they store it in a refrigerator today.

The iceman owned an icehouse where he stored the large chunks of ice he cut from frozen lakes and ponds in the winter. To keep the ice through the hot months of summer, he covered it with thick layers of sawdust. The sawdust insulated the ice even from the humid heat of July and August. The icehouse had no windows to let in warm sunlight, and it had a high roof where warm air could collect and flow through vents to the outside.

We still use insulation materials, though usually not sawdust, to prevent heat from escaping from our homes in the winter or to keep heat from entering them in the summer.

You can learn a lot about insulation by building ice cube keepers. If heat can't get to an ice cube easily, then the cube will melt slowly. You know how long it takes an ice cube to melt in air. Now, see how long you can keep it from melting in different insulated containers.

You might put the ice cube in a Styrofoam cup wrapped in newspaper. Or you might wrap it in sponges surrounded by glass wool. You could suspend the ice cubes on a string in a thermos bottle.

Fiberglass insulation like this retards the flow of heat through ceilings, walls, and floors.

Try these and other ways to keep an ice cube. Keep trying to improve your ice keeper.

You might even like to sponsor an ice cube-keeping contest with your classmates, your scout troop, or a club to which you belong. See who can keep an ice cube from melting the longest.

6. The Heat to Melt Ice

From the experiments you have done, you know that it takes a long time for ice to melt or water to freeze. You also know that while water is freezing or ice is melting, the temperature stays at 32°F (0°C). After all the water has frozen, the temperature of the ice falls to the temperature of the freezer. After all the ice has melted, the temperature of the water rises to that of its surroundings.

When you heat most substances, their temperature rises, but the temperature of melting ice remains at 32°F (0°C) throughout the melting process. Does this mean that *no* heat is needed to make ice melt? That doesn't seem right, does it? Certainly, ice melts faster when you hold it in your hands. You can feel your hands become colder as heat flows from your body to the ice.

Way back in the 1700s a Scottish chemist named Joseph Black designed an experiment to find out how much heat was required to melt a certain weight of ice. You can do an experiment that is very much like the one he did.

Pour one cup of water into one of two identical containers. Put the water into the freezer and leave it overnight so that it will be completely frozen when you start the experiment.

When you are ready to begin, mix some ice cubes and cold water in a pitcher to obtain ice water at 32°F (0°C). Remove the container of ice from the freezer and place it on a counter near the second container. When you see that the surface of the ice is beginning to melt, you will know that the ice temperature has risen to 32°F (0°C)—the temperature of the ice water in the pitcher. Pour one cup of ice water into the empty container beside the ice. Record the time, and place a thermometer in the ice water.

Watch the temperature of the ice water as it warms. How long does it take the ice water to warm to 40°F (4°C)?

How long does it take the ice to melt and warm up to 40°F (4°C)?

Can you figure out a way to determine the amount of heat needed to melt ice from the information you have collected? Can you figure out how many times as much heat is needed to melt ice as to warm an equal weight of ice water through 8°F (4°C)?

Now, compare your results with Joseph Black's. He assumed that since the ice and the ice water were in the same room, the same amount of heat would flow into both during the same time. In his experiment, it took ten and one-half hours for the ice to reach the temperature (40°F) attained by the ice water in one-half hour. Black reasoned that ten additional hours were needed for the ice to reach 40°F because of the extra heat needed to melt the ice. Therefore, he believed that it took twenty times as much heat to melt a pound of ice as it did to raise the temperature of a pound of water from 32°F to 40°F. (It took the ice ten hours to melt and one-half hour to warm up to 40°F after it became water.)

One way to measure heat is in Btu's (British thermal units). One Btu is the amount of heat needed to raise the temperature of one pound of water through one degree Fahrenheit. To raise the one-half pound of water in a cup of water through 8°F (from 32° to 40°) would require 4 Btu's (½ pound × 8°F = 4 Btu's). From his data, Joseph Black would have found that it takes 160 Btu's to melt one pound of ice (20 × 4 Btu's = 80 Btu's for ½ pound or 160 Btu's for 1 pound). More accurate experiments show that it takes 144 Btu's to melt one pound of ice. From your own results, how much heat, in Btu's, do you find is needed to melt one pound of ice?

You can measure heat in calories as well. A calorie is the amount of heat needed to raise the temperature of 1 gram of water through one degree Celsius. How much heat, in calories, is needed to melt 1 gram of ice?

CHAPTER

3

CHEMISTRY ON THE STOVE

Many chemical reactions occur only when substances are heated. Some of these reactions take place when we cook food, so it is fitting that as a kitchen chemist you use a stove for many experiments. **Be sure you have your parents' permission to use the stove. Stay alert to the dangers of fire. Use a pot holder to protect your hands when you touch a pan that has been heated. Perform experiments involving a stove or flame only in the presence of an adult.**

1. THE HEAT TO BOIL WATER

In Chapter 2 you found that it takes 144 Btu's of heat to melt one pound of ice. How much heat do you think it will take to boil away one pound of water?

Again, it was Joseph Black who first investigated this topic thoroughly. His method is one that you can try on the kitchen stove.

Measure the temperature of a pint of water, write down the temperature, and pour the water into a saucepan. Place the pan on one of the burners of your kitchen stove. (**Be careful and stay alert while you use the stove.**) **With the consent of an adult** turn on the heat, and record the time. How long does it take to bring the water to a boil? When the water is boiling, the temperature is about 212°F (100°C) unless you live at an altitude well above sea level.

How long does it take to boil away all the liquid once the water has reached the boiling temperature? **Be sure to remove the pan and turn off the stove** *as soon as* **the pan is empty.**

When Joseph Black did this experiment, he found that it took five minutes to warm the water from 50°F (10°C) to its boiling point. Another thirty minutes passed before all the water had changed to a gas (steam). He assumed the stove delivered the same amount of heat per minute to the water throughout the experiment. Thus, he found that it took six times as much heat to change the liquid water to gaseous water as it did to warm the water through 162°F (from 50°F to 212°F).

Had he used Btu's to measure heat, Joseph Black would have found that it took 162 Btu's to warm the pint of water from 50°F to the boiling point. A pint of water weighs one pound. A Btu, you'll remember, is the amount of heat needed to warm one pound of water through one degree Fahrenheit. To boil away one pound of water would have required six times as much heat, or 972 Btu's.

How do your results compare with those of Joseph Black?

How does the heat needed to change a pound of water to steam compare with the heat needed to convert a pound of ice to water?

2. HOT GAS, COLD GAS

From an earlier experiment (see Chapter 2, Experiment 1), you know that a gas shrinks when it cools. What do you think will happen to the volume of a gas when it is heated?

Put an empty balloon over the mouth of each of two 1-quart soft drink glass bottles. Leave one bottle at room temperature so you can compare it with a second bottle that is heated in a saucepan half filled with water. **With an adult present,** heat the pan on the stove until the water begins to boil. As soon as the water is boiling, turn off the heat. What happens to a volume of air when it is heated?

Does carbon dioxide gas behave the same way? How can you find out?

3. COIN CLATTER

You can hear as well as see an effect produced by air as it warms. Rinse an empty soda bottle with very cold water or leave the bottle in a refrigerator for a few minutes. After the air in the bottle has been cooled, use your finger to spread some water over the lip of the bottle's opening. Then place a coin that will cover the opening on the thin film of water. As the gas in the bottle warms, you will hear and see the coin click up and down.

What causes the coin to lift? How long will this clicking go on? Will the clicking rate increase if you put the bottle in bright sunlight? Will it increase if you place it in a pan of warm water?

4. CRUSHING A CAN WITH AIR PRESSURE

Many people can tell you that the pressure exerted by air at sea level is 14.7 pounds per square inch, but they don't realize the huge forces that can result from such a pressure. The total inward force on a cube one foot on each side is over *six tons*. Such a cube does not normally collapse because the air inside the cube exerts the same pressure as the air on the outside.

In this experiment, you'll see what happens when we get rid of the air that is normally inside a container.

Then you'll be able to see the effect of the force that air pressure exerts when there is no opposing force.

You will need a one-gallon metal can such as the kind that paint thinner or copy machine fluid comes in. If the can's screw-on cap is missing, you can use a rubber stopper that fits the opening in the can.

Rinse the can very thoroughly to remove any flammable liquid that might still remain. Pour a cup of water into the can. Leave the top of the can open, and **with an adult to help you,** place the can on a stove. When you heat the can, the steam produced as the water boils will replace the air that was inside the container. Let the water boil for several minutes to be sure that most of the air in the can has been replaced by steam.

Using gloves or a pot holder to protect your hands, remove the can from the heat and place it on a thick piece of cardboard or some other heatproof mat. *Immediately* seal the can with its screw-on cap or a rubber stopper.

Soon, as the can cools, the steam will condense, leaving the can nearly empty. Watch the air, unopposed now by air inside the can, push inward on all sides of the can. You'll be amazed how powerful air can be!

5. A SUPERSATURATED SOLUTION

A saturated solution has dissolved in it all the solute it can hold at a particular temperature. But sometimes more solute can be dissolved than would normally be found in a saturated solution. Such a solution is *super-saturated,* and you can make one quite easily.

Buy some hypo (sodium thiosulfate) crystals from a photography shop, or ask your science teacher if you may use some from the school's laboratory.

Fill a small juice glass or test tube about one-quarter full with hypo crystals. Place the glass or test tube in a small pan of water, and, **with an adult to help you,** heat the pan on the stove until the solid turns into a liquid. There is enough water in the hypo crystals to dissolve the solid at temperatures close to 200°F (90°C). When all the solid has dissolved, stir the hypo solution with a spoon or straw and turn off the stove.

Use a glove or pot holder to remove the glass or test tube. Let the solution cool to room temperature. Since hypo is more soluble in hot water than in cold water, you may have a saturated solution after it has cooled down to room temperature.

To see if the solution is supersaturated, add a *tiny* crystal of hypo to the solution. What happens? How do you know that the solution was supersaturated?

If you have a magnifying glass, you will enjoy seeing the crystals grow around the tiny "seed" crystal. It's a beautiful sight.

6. Growing Crystals

Crystals will emerge from a saturated solution only if we cool or evaporate water from the solution. If the water in such a solution evaporates slowly in the presence of a seed crystal, it is possible to grow large, beautiful crystals.

To prepare a saturated solution of potassium alum, begin by adding one-half teaspoon of the solid to one-quarter glass of water. (You can obtain alum from your school or pharmacy.) Stir until all the solid dissolves. Continue to add alum a half-teaspoon at a time until no more solid will dissolve even after thorough stirring. How do you know this solution is saturated?

Put the glass of solution into some water in a saucepan, and heat the pan until the water boils. (**Be sure an adult is present.**) Do you think the solution in the glass is still saturated?

To find out, see if you can dissolve another one-half teaspoon of alum in the warm solution. Add three more teaspoons and see if you can stir this additional solid into solution.

Turn off the heat and, **using a glove or pot holder to protect your hand,** remove the glass of hot solution from the pan. Pour the solution into a Styrofoam cup so that it will cool slowly. Suspend a paper clip from the center of a length of thread and hang it in the coffee cup as shown in Figure 13. A second cup, from which you have cut away the upper third, can be used to hold the thread firmly against the cup that contains the hot solution.

Leave the solution to cool for a day. When you return, you should find tiny alum crystals on the thread.

Why would you expect crystals to form as this solution cools?

If there are no crystals, gently swirl the liquid in the cup. This disturbance of the supersaturated solution should cause crystals to begin forming on the thread within a few minutes.

Remove the thread and paper clip from the solution. Pour the solution, but none of the crystals that may be on the bottom of the cup, into another clean container. Pull away all but one of the crystals on the thread. Tie the thread to a paper clip that has been straightened out and placed across the top of the cup. The crystal should hang in the middle of the solution. Watch it grow as the solution slowly evaporates.

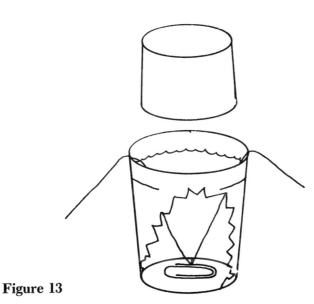

Figure 13

7. CARBON DIOXIDE AND BAKING

Carbon dioxide is a baker's friend. To see why, make two small cakes. Make the first cake by mixing flour and warm water until you have a smooth dough. Prepare the second cake by mixing three parts flour with one part baking powder. Then add warm water.

Put both cakes in a small greased pan and **ask an adult to help you** heat the pan on the kitchen stove. When you think the cakes are done, turn off the heat and let them cool.

How do the two cakes compare? Break open both cakes. In which cake was carbon dioxide produced? How can you tell? Where do you think the carbon dioxide gas came from?

To see that baking powder is a source of carbon dioxide, cover the bottom of a pint-size peanut butter jar with baking powder. Add some hot tap water to the jar and watch the bubbles of carbon dioxide form in the solution.

To see that the bubbles are carbon dioxide, pour the gas from the jar onto a burning birthday candle as you did in Chapter 1, Experiment 22. What evidence do you have that the gas is carbon dioxide?

8. INVISIBLE INK

One type of invisible ink used by detectives in mystery stories can be prepared by a kitchen chemist.

The secret ingredient is lemon juice. Just squeeze a little into a cup. Dip a toothpick or watercolor paintbrush into the lemon juice, and write a message on a file card.

When the lemon-juice ink dries, it leaves a thin deposit of fine white crystals. These crystals are mostly citric acid, a solid found in lemons and other citrus fruits. The fine crystals are very difficult to see, but when the citric acid is heated, it changes to carbon (a black element) and other colored substances. So you can make the writing on the card visible by heating it. **Before you heat the card, ask an adult to help you.** Also, place a large pan of water near or on the stove. Should the card accidentally catch fire, you can plunge it into the water.

When the "ink" is dry, hold the card with kitchen tongs and carefully move it back and forth above the heating element or burner on the kitchen stove. Keep it high enough above the flame or coil so that it does not char or burn. If it begins to scorch, raise it higher above the heat. The invisible message you wrote can now be read easily.

9. MAKING THE VISIBLE INVISIBLE

The message that you made visible by heating can be made invisible again by some more kitchen chemistry. Simply dip a folded facial tissue into some liquid bleach and blot (don't rub) the writing gently with the damp tissue. Watch the visible become invisible again!

Liquid bleach is poisonous. Keep it away from your

Invisible ink makes mysterious writing appear.

nose and mouth. **Wash your hands thoroughly after you finish blotting away the message.**

Bleaches contain a chemical that will react with many colored substances to form colorless substances. Sometimes these colorless materials can be changed back to their colored form by heating.

Can you make the message reappear by heating the card again? Or has the invisible ink been permanently removed by the bleach? Ask an adult to help you heat the card. Take all the precautions you took the first time you heated the card.

10. Making Real Ink Disappear

Can the same bleach you used in Experiment 9 make a dark, inky solution turn clear? Can it make a message written in normal, visible ink disappear?

Add a drop or two of black ink to some water in a glass and stir to mix. Now add a few drops of liquid bleach to the dark mixture. (**Remember that the bleach is poisonous! Handle with care.**) Stir for a minute or two, and the liquid will turn clear if you've added enough bleach.

How many drops of bleach are required to clear up one drop of ink in water?

Can the same bleach on a facial tissue be used to blot away a letter written with a felt-tip pen? Can it be used to blot away a letter written with a ball point pen?

Be sure to wash and rinse your hands and all glass-ware used in this experiment.

A PREDICTION: See if you can predict how many drops of bleach will be needed to clear up two drops of ink in water.

Were you right?

Can you predict how many drops will be needed to clear up three drops of ink in water? To clear up four drops of ink?

11. MORE INVISIBLE "INK"

Here's a method for writing with invisible ink that's used to make the watermarks for identifying postage stamps. Dip a small sheet of paper into a pan of water. Place the wet paper on a hard, smooth surface such as a Formica®-covered kitchen counter. Put a dry piece of paper on top of the wet one and write a message on the dry paper with a ball point pen. Bear down hard as you write so that the wet paper fibers underneath are crushed by the pressure you apply.

Separate the two sheets of paper and put the wet sheet aside. When it has dried, the message you wrote will be very hard to see. If you wet the paper and hold it so that it reflects light, the words can be easily seen. The smoothed, crushed fibers under the message you wrote reflect light better than the rest of the paper when wet.

12. A Salty Hidden Message

Prepare a small amount of salt solution using salt and warm water. Dissolve as much salt as you can. Dip the broad end of a toothpick into the salt solution and use it as a pen to write a message on a sheet of paper. Dip your "pen" into the salty "ink" often to be sure plenty of salt gets onto the paper.

After the liquid has thoroughly dried, the message remains invisible. To read what was written you can gently rub the paper with the side of the graphite in a soft pencil. Rub in different directions. You'll hear a scratchy sound when you're moving the pencil in the right direction over the salt in a particular letter.

13. Disappearing Glass

When light passes from air to water, glass, diamond, or any other transparent material, it is bent. You can see this for yourself. Fill a plain, clear drinking glass or plastic cylinder with water. Put a pencil into the glass and look at the pencil from the side. You will see that the pencil appears to be broken at the point where it enters the water. Light passing from the pencil through the water is bent when it emerges into air.

Another way to see this effect is to place a coin on the bottom of a teacup as shown in Figure 14. Lower your head so that the coin just disappears from your view. Ask someone to slowly pour some water into the cup. The coin will become visible again.

If two substances bend light coming from air through the same angle, one will become invisible if placed in the other. Because the two substances behave in the same way with respect to light, light passing from one to the other will not be bent or reflected. Therefore, if one object is placed inside the other, light goes right through the one inside without being affected in any way.

Cooking oil and Pyrex glass bend light coming from air through the same angle. Consequently, Pyrex glass will disappear if placed in cooking oil. If possible, borrow a few short lengths of Pyrex glass tubing from your school. Place the short lengths of tubing in a clear glass of cooking oil. You will see the tubing slowly disappear as the air in the tubes becomes filled with cooking oil.

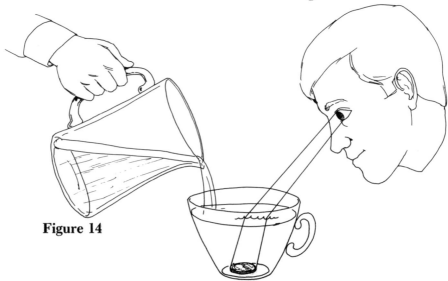

Figure 14

CHEMISTRY ON THE KITCHEN COUNTER

One thing that every experimental scientist needs is space to conduct research. Almost every kitchen has a counter or a table where experiments can be carried out. The experiments in this chapter do not require heat or ice. You can do them on a counter or table, but you will need water and some chemicals and other materials that may be stored in cabinets about the kitchen and elsewhere.

1. IODINE TO INK—A TEST FOR STARCH

One test that chemists and biologists use to determine the presence of starch is to add an iodine solution to a solid or liquid that is suspected to contain starch.

To see what happens when starch and iodine react, you will need to prepare an iodine solution. You can do this by adding about twenty drops of tincture of iodine to a glass of water. (**Iodine is *poisonous* so keep it away from your mouth and be sure to wash your hands and all glassware and utensils when you finish this experiment.**)

Now that you have a solution of iodine, pour about half of it into a glass with about one-half teaspoon of cornstarch. Stir the mixture. The dark blue color tells you that starch is present.

To see if some foods contain starch, add a few drops of the iodine solution to small pieces of bread, cake, and raw potato. Try adding drops of the iodine solution to some powders in medicine cups or small aluminum pans. You might test sugar, flour, baking soda, and salt in addition to cornstarch. Which of these substances contain starch?

2. ACIDS AND BASES

Chemists divide substances into groups. There are solids, liquids, and gases; there are mixtures and pure substances; there are elements and compounds; and there are acids, bases, and neutral substances.

Acids contain hydrogen, have a sour taste, react with metals such as zinc to form hydrogen gas, react with bases to produce salts and water, and conduct electricity when they dissolve in water.

Bases have a bitter taste, react with acids to form

salts and water, and conduct electricity when they dissolve in water.

A substance such as water that appears to be neither an acid nor a base is said to be neutral.

Both acids and bases change the color of certain chemicals called indicators. For example, litmus, a purple material obtained from lichens, turns red in acids and blue in basic solutions.

To see how indicators help you identify acids and bases, you can use litmus paper if you have any at home or in school. If not, you can use unsweetened grape juice as an indicator. Grape juice is red in an acid, but turns green in a basic solution. **You will need household ammonia for this experiment. Ask your parents' permission to use it and wash your hands afterward.**

Place a few drops of household ammonia in a glass or a medicine cup. Dip a piece of red litmus paper into the ammonia or add a drop of grape juice. Is ammonia an acid or a base?

A PREDICTION: What do you think will happen if you hold a piece of moist red litmus paper *over* the ammonia solution?

Place a few drops of vinegar in a glass or medicine cup, and again test with litmus paper or a drop of grape juice. Is vinegar an acid or a base?

Vinegar is a dilute solution of acetic acid. Can it be neutralized by the basic ammonia solution?

To find out, add ammonia drop by drop to the vinegar until the red litmus turns blue, or until drops of the grape juice turn green.

See if you can predict how many ounces of vinegar you will need to neutralize an ounce of the household ammonia you used before. To neutralize the ammonia means to remove its basic properties by allowing it to react with acid until it has changed to salt and water.

Add a few drops of grape juice to a fluid ounce (30 ml) of ammonia. Then pour measured volumes of vinegar into the ammonia solution until the color quickly changes from green to red.

Did you predict the volume needed correctly?

Using grape juice or litmus as an indicator, find out if the following are acidic, basic, or neutral: water, lemon juice, orange juice, a solution of scouring powder, baking soda in water, a strong soap solution, soda water, tea, and aspirin in water.

Add a few drops of grape juice to an ounce of vinegar in a glass. Can you neutralize the acidic vinegar by adding baking soda?

A PREDICTION: Add about ½ ounce (15 ml) of grape juice to 5 ounces (150 ml) of water in a glass. If the mixture is not green, add ammonia drop by drop until it turns green. What do you predict will happen if you add an Alka-Seltzer® tablet to the green solution?

3. BOUNCING BUTTONS

In the last experiment, you saw bubbles of gas form-

Buttons aren't the only things that will rise when associated with a gas. Notice how this huge fuel tank is strapped to the concrete base on which it rests. If this were not done, an empty, air-filled tank might be pushed up through the earth by water in the surrounding soil during a wet season.

ing when you added baking soda (sodium bicarbonate) to vinegar. These same bubbles of carbon dioxide gas are found in carbonated beverages such as cola, ginger ale, and soda water. The bubbles can be used to lift a button.

Pour some ginger ale or soda water from a freshly opened bottle into a clear glass. Drop a small button into the liquid. It will sink, but it will soon rise to the surface, rest for a few seconds, and then sink once more.

As long as there are carbon dioxide bubbles in the liquid, the button will continue to bounce up and down in the glass. If the bouncing button begins to lose its tempo, simply add a little more ginger ale to the glass.

To see why the button bounces as it does, watch closely as it settles on the bottom. Notice that the gas bubbles stick to the sunken button. As bubbles collect on the button, they make the combination of bubbles and button lighter than an equal volume of water. As a result, the button with its attached bubbles rise to the surface.

Watch the button as it rests on the surface. Why does it sink again?

See if you can make the button bounce using baking soda and vinegar. Will the button bounce if the carbon dioxide bubbles come from Alka-Seltzer®?

4. DANCING RAISINS

Buttons are not the only things that will bounce

about in carbonated beverages. Pieces of raisins will "dance" nicely in a glass of cola or soda water.

To see the dance of the raisins, cut several raisins into quarters, and add them to a freshly poured glass of ginger ale or club soda.

Look closely! Can you find tiny gas bubbles clinging to the raisins? Why do you think the raisins do their peculiar dance in the liquid? Would they dance in a glass of water? In a glass of hot water fresh from the faucet?

5. A Leaping Flame

To see a flame leap, you are going to have to use matches. **Because matches are dangerous, you should ask a parent or other adult to help you with this experiment.** The adult will enjoy the experiment as much as you will.

Place a candle in a holder or on a metal lid and light it. After the candle has burned for several minutes, light another match and blow out the candle. Bring the match to the stream of white smoke that rises from the extinguished candle. (See Figure 15.) You will find that the flame will follow the smoke stream back to the wick and ignite the candle again. The flame seems to leap from the match down to the wick.

Repeat this experiment several times. How far can you get the flame to jump?

Figure 15

6. A Burning Candle

In this investigation of what makes a candle burn, you will again be using matches. **Ask a parent or other adult to help you as you do these experiments.**

Light a candle that has been used and is not very tall. Watch it burn. How many colors do you see in the flame? What is the shape of the flame? Where does the flame begin and end?

You can't get inside the flame to see that there is no burning there, but you can do an experiment that will show you that burning occurs along the outside of the flame.

Hold a glass partly filled with water well above the flame. When the flame is burning steadily and evenly, lower the bottom of the glass into the flame's center for about one second. (See Figure 16.) Lift the glass out of the flame and you will see a ring of soot where the flame was burning.

Look closely at the wick of a candle that is not burning. Use a magnifying glass if you have one. You can see that the wick is made up of threads woven together. Melted candle wax will move up the spaces between these threads just as water ascends through the narrow openings between the wood fibers of a paper towel. (Remember Experiment 4 in Chapter 1?)

You can see that melted wax flows toward the wick of a burning candle. Just add a few tiny particles of soot to the outer edge of the pool of wax below the

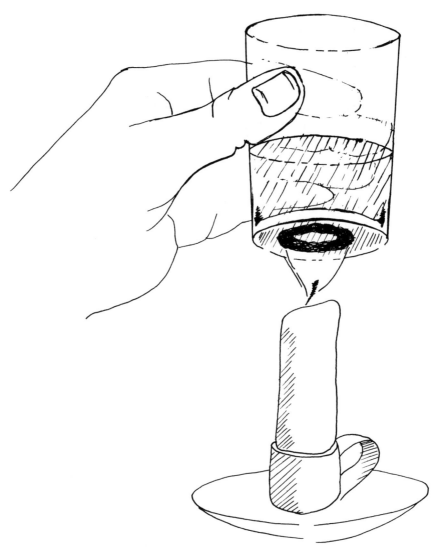

Figure 16

flame. You can get the soot by using a toothpick to scrape off some of the black ring from the glass you lowered into the flame. Dip the sooty end of the toothpick into the outer edge of the melted wax. Watch the tiny black specks, carried by the flowing wax, move toward the wick.

What would happen if there were no tiny spaces inside the wick? Would the candle still burn?

To find out, use a pin to make a small hole in the side of a candle. Break a wooden toothpick in half and insert it into the hole as shown in Figure 17. Light the toothpick to see if it will serve as a wick.

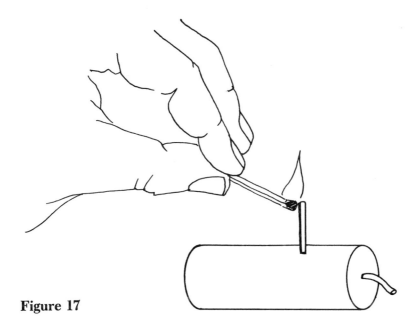

Figure 17

Can toothpicks be used as wicks?

Here is yet another way to show that liquid wax ascends the tiny spaces within the wick of a burning candle. With a medicine dropper, place one or two drops of water near the edge of the pool of liquid wax at the base of the candle flame. Because water is heavier (for the same volume) than wax, the water will flow under the hot wax. What do you think will happen as the water reaches and ascends the wick? Watch and see if you are right.

The wax that nourishes the flame cannot move up the wick unless it is liquid. Where do you think the heat needed to melt the wax comes from?

What will happen if you reflect the heat away from the candle flame? You can find out by sliding a slit piece of aluminum foil (a good heat reflector) around the wick

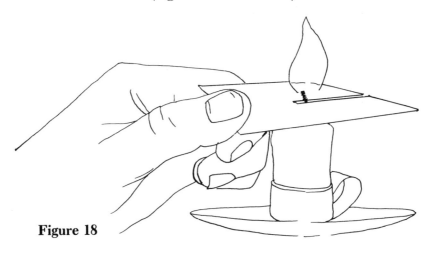

Figure 18

just below the flame but above the pool of wax as shown in Figure 18.

Why do you think the flame goes out after a minute or so?

A PREDICTION: Will a thick candle always produce a bigger flame than a thin candle? Test your prediction with candles of various sizes. What do you find? What does determine the size of the candle's flame?

7. CANDLES AND AIR

Would a giant candle burn for days in a room so well sealed that no fresh air could enter? It's difficult to build such a room, but you can see what happens in a small sealed "room."

This is another experiment that requires matches and flames, so you should **get a parent or other adult to work with you.**

Light a birthday candle. When it is burning well, tip the candle so that a few drops of melted wax fall on a tin can lid. Put the base of the candle into the melted wax to fasten it to the metal lid.

Turn a pint glass jar upside down and lower it over the burning candle. (See Figure 19.) How long does the candle burn in this pint-sized room? How long do you think the candle will burn in a quart-sized room? How long will it burn if you cover it with a gallon jar?

Figure 19

8. Oxygen and a Burning Candle

How much of the oxygen in a closed space does a candle use up before it goes out? This experiment will help you find out, but again **you'll need an adult to help as you light matches and use flames.**

To do this experiment you will need one or more tall, thin jars like the kind olives come in. You will

94

also need birthday candles, steel wool, clay, water, matches, and vinegar. Most steel wool comes in packages that hold six large rolls. From one roll you can make about a dozen small, loosely rolled balls of steel wool for this experiment. "Pickle" the steel-wool balls by soaking them overnight in a jar that contains one part white vinegar and two parts water. The pickling process will remove the protective coating on the steel.

Remove one of the pickled steel-wool balls from the jar and shake it dry over the sink. Push the steel-wool ball to the bottom of a tall, narrow jar. Turn the jar upside down and place it in a pan of shallow water as shown in Figure 20a. Iron in the steel combines with the oxygen above the water in the jar. You will see the water level rise in the jar. The water replaces the oxygen that has combined with the iron to form iron oxide (rust). (Figure 20b.) After twenty-four hours, mark the water level in the jar. What fraction of the air in the jar was oxygen? (Assume that all the oxygen in the jar combined with the iron.)

Repeat the experiment several times. Are the results the same for each trial?

Use a small piece of clay to support a birthday candle. Place the candle in some shallow water in a container. Light the candle. Then cover it with the tall, narrow jar you used to see how much of the air would react with steel wool. (Figure 21.) As you can see, water rises up the jar, but did you see bubbles of expanding air emerge from the bottom of the jar?

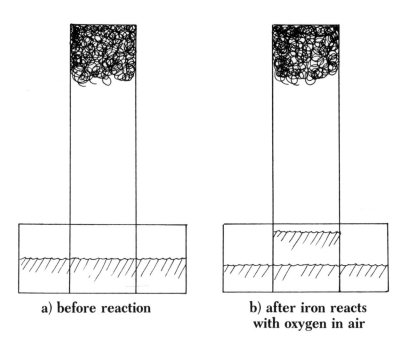

a) before reaction

b) after iron reacts
with oxygen in air

Figure 20

Does the water rise up in the jar because the burning candle uses up all the oxygen from the air as it burns out or because the cooling air occupies less volume than it did when it was heated by the candle? What fraction of the air in the jar has been replaced by water?

Repeat the experiment several times. Does the water always rise to the same level in the jar?

Put a little soap or detergent in the shallow water and repeat the experiment. Can you see bubbles of gas forming at the mouth of the jar when it is placed over

the burning candle? What could explain the presence
of these bubbles?

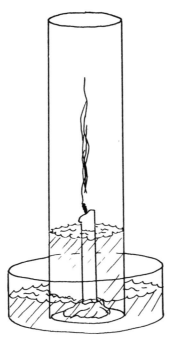

**Figure 21.   Did the candle use up *all* the oxygen in the
jar?**

Repeat the experiment, but this time put a ball of
steel wool in the bottom of the tall, thin jar. (See Figure
22.) Mark the water level in the jar after the candle
goes out and the water stops rising. After twenty-four
hours, check the water level in the jar again. Did the
candle use up all the oxygen in the jar when it burned?

What made the water level rise higher in the jar during the twenty-four-hour period? How does the water level rise during the twenty-four hours after the candle went out compare with the rise when there was only steel wool in the tube?

Perhaps the water level will rise in any tube in which a candle has burned. To find out, invert a jar over a burning candle. When the water stops rising,

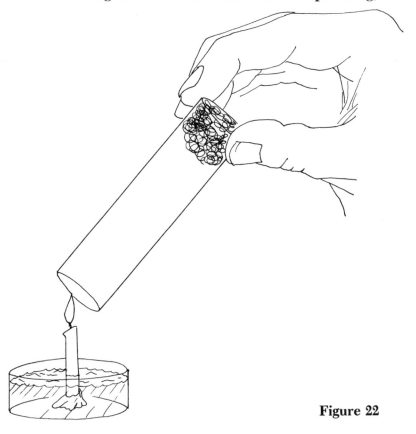

Figure 22

mark its level with a rubber band, tape, or a marking pen, and leave the jar for twenty-four hours. Does the water level change very much?

What fraction of air seems to be oxygen?

What fraction of the oxygen in air is used by a burning candle before it goes out?

9. COLORED LIQUIDS THAT SINK OR FLOAT

Make a saturated salt solution by adding 60 to 70 grams of salt (20 to 25 tsp.) to 7 fluid ounces (200 ml) of water. Continue to add salt, if necessary, until no more will dissolve. If possible, use kosher salt. Remember that most ordinary table salts have added ingredients that make their solutions cloudy. You'll probably need 40 to 50 teaspoons of the kosher variety to make a saturated solution.

Pour the saturated solution into another container to separate it from any undissolved salt.

Pour *half* of the saturated solution (about 3½ oz., or 100 ml) into a second container. Dilute this portion by adding to it an equal volume of water (3½ oz., or 100 ml).

Pour half of this diluted solution into a third container. Dilute this liquid still further by adding an equal volume (3½ oz., or 100 ml) of water.

You now have three solutions: one is saturated; the second has half as much salt per volume of liquid as the first; the third has only one-fourth as much salt per volume of liquid as the first.

To identify these different solutions, add a few drops of green food coloring to the first, or saturated, solution. Color the second solution with red food coloring. Make the third, or least concentrated, solution blue.

Obtain four clear pill vials or medicine cups. Put them side by side on the kitchen counter. Fill the first vial about three-fourths full with the green (saturated) salt solution. Pour some of the red solution into the second vial; add some blue solution to the third vial. Pour plain water into the fourth vial. If you want a fourth color, add a couple of drops of yellow food coloring to the water.

Use a medicine dropper to remove some of the red solution from the second vial. Place the tip of the dropper in the middle of the water in the fourth vial. *Gently* squeeze a little of the red solution out into the water, as shown in Figure 23. Does the red liquid sink or rise in the water?

Repeat the experiment in the blue liquid. Does the red liquid rise or sink when it is squeezed gently into the blue solution? What happens when the red liquid flows from the medicine dropper into the green liquid? Does it rise or sink?

What will happen if you gently squeeze a drop of green solution into each of the other three liquids? How about drops of the blue solution in the other liquids? In which liquids does the blue liquid sink? In which

Figure 23

one(s) does it rise? Can you predict what will happen if you squeeze a little water from the fourth vial into the other three liquids?

A PREDICTION: Which of these four liquids do you think is the heaviest; that is, which one weighs the most if you weigh equal volumes of all four? If you have a balance or scale (see Experiment 4 in Chapter 2) you can test your predictions by using the same container to weigh equal volumes—say, 3 or 4 fluid ounces (about 100 ml) of each liquid.

Save your colored liquids for the next experiment.

10. Colored-Liquid Layers

A *pipette* can be used to pick up and move liquids. You can make your own pipette from a straw. And with a transparent plastic straw, you can make layers of colored liquids.

Begin by perfecting your technique in lifting liquids. Place a straw in some water. Put your index finger over the upper end of the straw and lift the straw from the water. (See Figure 24.) Air pressure holds the water in the straw. Lift your finger, and the pressure at both ends of the liquid becomes equal. The water flows out of the straw.

Once you are good at moving liquids with your see-through straw, you can make a two-layered, colored-liquid "cake" in the straw.

Dip the straw a short way into a vial of the blue liquid you prepared in Experiment 9. Put your finger over the straw and lift it out of the liquid. Keeping your finger over the top of the straw, place the straw and the blue liquid within it into the red solution. Push the straw deep enough into the liquid so that the blue liquid in the straw is lower than the surface of the red liquid in the vial. Then release your finger. Red liquid will enter the straw pushing the blue liquid upward until it is even with the surface of the red liquid in the vial.

Now put your finger back on the top of the straw and lift the straw out of the red liquid. Look! You have

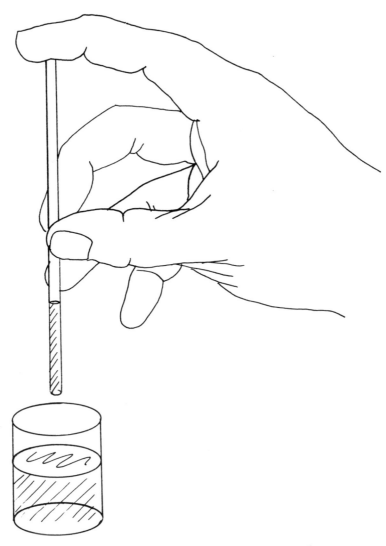

Figure 24.   You can use a straw to move liquids.

made a two-layered, colored-liquid "cake"—blue on top of red!

Why can't you make a two-layered cake with the red liquid on top of the blue?

How many two-layered cakes can you make from the four liquids? How many three-layered cakes can you prepare? Can you make a four-layered cake?

Using rubbing alcohol and cooking oil as well as the other four liquids, how many two-, three-, and four-layered cakes can you make? Can you make five-layered cakes? How many? Can you make a six-layered cake? Which liquid is always the top layer? Which liquid is always the bottom layer?

List these six liquids according to their heaviness (weight for the same volume). Put the lightest liquid at the top and the heaviest liquid at the bottom of your list.

Using your method of making liquid layers, see if you can place some of the following liquids in their proper slots on your heaviness list: cranberry juice, apple juice, vinegar, salad oil, syrup, and grape juice.

From what you have learned, make liquid layers in a vial or medicine cup using an eyedropper to move liquids.

A prediction: If you make a two-layered, colored-liquid cake and then turn the straw upside down, will the layers remain separated? What will happen when you turn the straw right side up again?

11. FALLING BALLOONS

Do balloons filled with different gases fall at the same or different speeds in air? What is your guess?

To test your hunch, blow up one balloon with carbon dioxide; blow up another with air.

To fill a balloon with carbon dioxide, break two Alka-Seltzer® tablets into small pieces. Add them to

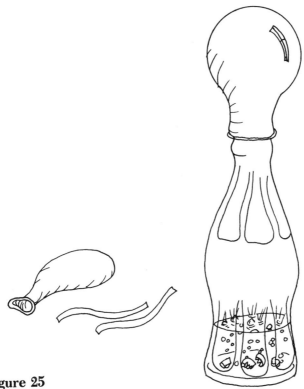

Figure 25

about an ounce of water in a small soft drink bottle, and immediately put the neck of a balloon over the mouth of the bottle as in Figure 25. When the Alka-Seltzer® stops reacting with water to make carbon dioxide gas, remove the balloon and tie it off with a tie band.

Using a tire or balloon pump, fill a second identical balloon with air. Adjust the size of this balloon by adding or letting out air until it is the same size as the carbon dioxide-filled balloon. Seal its neck with a tie band.

Hold the two balloons well above the floor and let go of both of them at the same time. Which balloon falls faster? Repeat the experiment several times. Does the carbon dioxide balloon always fall faster?

Fill a third balloon with air from your lungs until it is the same size as the other two balloons. Wipe away any saliva that may be on the mouth of the balloon. Seal its neck with another tie band. Will this balloon fall faster, more slowly, or at the same speed as the carbon dioxide balloon? What do you predict?

Were you right?

How do you think the falling speed of the balloon filled with your lung air will compare with that of the air-filled balloon? Try it!

Does "lung air" seem to be more like carbon dioxide or ordinary air?

Save these balloons for the next experiment.

12. Do Balloons Leak?

Using a tape measure, find the circumference (distance around) of each of the three balloons you used in Experiment 11.

Leave the three balloons in a safe place. Examine them after a few hours and after several days. Do any of the balloons seem to leak? Does any one appear to leak more than another?

Place a few drops of perfume in a balloon. Wipe away any liquid from the mouth of the balloon. Then fill the balloon using a bicycle tire pump or a balloon pump. Seal the balloon with a tie band. After a few minutes, sniff along the balloon's surface. Do you smell perfume? Can perfume vapor get through the balloon?

Ask an adult to help you place a few drops of household ammonia solution in another balloon using an eyedropper. Use a pump to fill this balloon with air and seal it off with a tie band. After a few minutes, sniff along the surface of this balloon. Does ammonia gas come through the balloon?

13. Electrical Conductors and Non-Conductors

When electricity flows through the light bulbs and appliances in your home, it moves along metal wires of different kinds and thicknesses. But for electricity to flow through an automobile battery, it must move through the liquids in the cells that make up a battery. Solids and liquids through which electricity moves easily are called conductors; materials that do not allow electricity to flow are called nonconductors.

You can test different things to see if they are conductors by placing them in a circuit that has a flashlight bulb. As you may know, to make a bulb light, one lead from a battery has to touch the side of the metal base just below the glass part of the bulb (1 in Figure 26). The other pole of the battery must be connected to the small piece of metal at the very bottom of the bulb

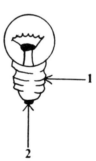

Figure 26

(2 in Figure 26). See if you can light a flashlight bulb with a D-cell flashlight battery and a wire.

To make a conductivity tester, you will need four D-cells, a mailing tube an inch or two shorter than the four D-cells lined up end to end, a strong, wide rubber band that will go around the mailing tube lengthwise, two pieces of wire or paper clips, some masking tape, and a flashlight bulb.

Place the D-cells end to end inside the mailing tube. The plus (+) pole of one cell should touch the minus (−) pole of the next cell. Hold the four cells tightly together by placing the wide, strong rubber band around the cells and mailing tube. Use the two pieces of wire to connect the bulb to the two poles, plus and minus, at the ends of the four-cell battery. By coiling the ends of the wires, you can probably make better contact between the wires and the battery poles. You might have to tape the ends of the wires to the battery poles. (See Figure 27.)

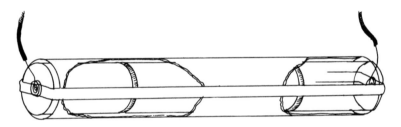

Figure 27. A four-cell battery.

Use a little tape to hold one wire lead from the battery to the side of the metal base of the bulb. (Figure 28.) Touch the other battery lead wire to the metal at the very bottom of the bulb. The bulb should light. Don't leave it connected for more than a second; the bulb might burn out!

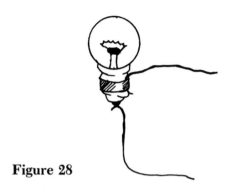

Figure 28

To test various solids to see if they are conductors, hold one lead from the battery firmly against one end of the solid. *Briefly* touch the metal tip at the base of the bulb to the other end of the solid as shown in Figure 29. If the bulb lights, you know the solid is a conductor of electricity.

Test a variety of things: silverware, nails, plastic, pencils and pencil lead, wood, paper, wax, and so forth. Which are conductors? Which are nonconductors?

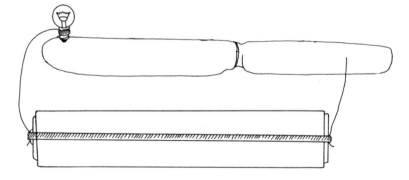

Figure 29

To test the conductivity of liquids, slide two paper clips over the edge of a medicine cup filled with the liquid you want to test. At least the lower half of both paper clips should be in the liquid. Slide one lead wire from the battery under the part of a paper clip that is outside the cup. The tip at the base of the bulb can be held firmly against the top of the other paper clip. The two clips should be close but not touching each other so that electricity must pass through the liquid to move from one clip to the other. (See Figure 30.)

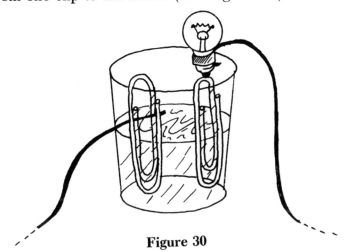

Figure 30

Try testing such liquids as water; milk; lemon juice; vinegar; saturated solutions of salt, sugar, and baking soda; and so forth. How can you tell which liquids are conductors of electricity?

Repeat your tests for the liquid nonconductors. In some instances you may find that even though the bulb does not light, gas bubbles up around the paper clips. This suggests that while there is not enough electricity to light the bulb, there is enough to cause some kind of chemical reaction around the electrodes (paper clips) in the liquid.

14. ELECTRICITY FROM FRUITS AND VEGETABLES

A battery or electric cell contains chemicals and electrodes. In a flashlight cell a carbon rod immersed in the center of the cell serves as the positive (+) electrode. The casing of the cell, which is made of zinc, is the negative (−) electrode. Inside the cell is a damp mixture of manganese dioxide, ammonium chloride, and powdered carbon—an electrolyte—that conducts electric charge though the cell. Electric cells of this type are quite safe by themselves. **Do not experiment with electrical devices that plug into electric outlets. The electricity associated with such plugs can be very dangerous.**

For homemade fruit and vegetable cells you can use copper, aluminum, and iron nails as well as strips of zinc and other metals as electrodes. The contents of the fruits will serve as the electrolytes. To measure the electrical energy produced by your cells, you will need a galvanometer. You can probably borrow one from your school. If not, you can make one by winding about 2 or 3 yards (meters) of enameled copper wire around a compass needle as shown in Figure 31. Sand away the

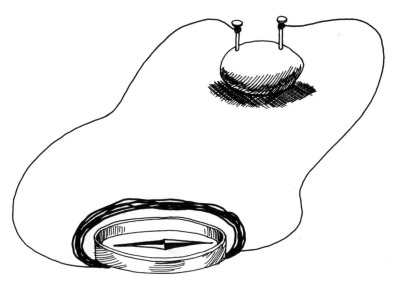

Figure 31.   A homemade galvanometer.

insulating enamel from the ends of the wires and connect them to the electrodes of your cell.

You might begin by placing a zinc and a copper electrode in a large olive. Connect one end of the wire from the galvanometer to the copper electrode and the other end to the zinc electrode. Does your meter indicate that any electrical current is produced? You can use other fruits or vegetables as electrolytes too. You might try lemons, apples, oranges, pickles, potatoes, tomatoes, etc.

Which fruit or vegetable makes the best electrolyte? Which pair of different metal electrodes provide the greatest amount of electrical current?

Hold the best pair of electrodes in your hands while they are connected to the galvanometer. Is your body an electrolyte? Are you a better electrolyte if your hands are damp? Do you see why it is dangerous to touch electrical devices while in the bathtub?

CHAPTER
5
CHEMISTRY ALL AROUND THE KITCHEN

Many experiments require the use of a sink, water, heat, ice, counter space, and various instruments and vessels. For the experiments that follow, you will move about the kitchen and use a variety of appliances and materials. These experiments are a bit more complicated than any you've done before, but by now you're such a practiced scientist that you should have no difficulty. In fact, you'll find fewer instructions in this chapter because you are now ready to design many of your own experiments.

1. WHITE-POWDER CHEMISTRY

If you've ever spread salt instead of sugar on your breakfast cereal, you know that many white powders in the kitchen look alike. But there are ways to tell them apart without tasting. Tasting could be dangerous because lye, the poisonous substance used to clean clogged drains, is also a white powder.

Looking

Put some starch, flour, sugar, salt, and baking soda into separate, labeled containers. Put a spoon in each white powder so that you can remove samples of each without mixing them.

Use a magnifier to look closely at a small sample of each white powder. Do the samples look alike? Could you tell one powder from another just by looking closely?

Smelling

Can you distinguish among the white solids by their odors? **Careful! Don't inhale the powders!**

Feeling

Do the different powders feel the same when you rub them between your fingers? Could you identify the powders by touching them if your eyes were closed?

Dissolving

Which white solids dissolve in water? Are some more soluble than others? Do any of them seem to be more soluble in hot water than in cold water? Are any of the powders insoluble in water?

To test their solubility more carefully, stir a teaspoonful of one powder into an ounce of water. Then pour the mixture through a paper-towel filter (see Chapter 1, Experiment 14). Collect the liquid on a saucer as it comes through the filter. Label the saucer and set it aside to dry in a warm place.

After rinsing your stirring spoon, repeat the process with each of the other white powders.

Examine each saucer closely when the material has dried. Which saucers indicate that the white powder tested was soluble in water? How can you tell? Which saucers indicate that the powder was nearly insoluble in water?

Testing with Iodine

Place a quarter-teaspoon of each powder in separate, labeled glass, plastic, or porcelain containers. (Do *not* use paper cups or plates for this experiment.) Prepare an iodine solution to test these powders by adding one or two drops of tincture of iodine to 60 drops of water. (**Remember that iodine is poisonous!**) With an eyedropper, add several drops of the iodine solution you have made to each sample of white solid. What happens to each powder? Which solids could you identify by adding an iodine solution?

To see why you should not use paper containers, add a drop of iodine solution to samples of several different kinds of white paper. What happens with at least some of the papers you tested? Which white powder is an ingredient in at least some paper? How can you tell?

Heating

Perhaps you can distinguish among some of these solids by heating them.

To find out, place about one-half teaspoon of each powder on the bottom of an aluminum pie or cake pan. Leave plenty of room between the powders and arrange them in a pattern so that you can remember where each powder is. A labeled diagram may prove helpful.

Ask an adult to help you put the pan on the stove and heat the powders. Do any of the powders melt? Do any seem to change to something else?

Which powders can you identify by heating?

Use kitchen tongs or a pot holder to remove the hot pan.

Testing with Vinegar

Place one-fourth teaspoon of each powder in a small, separate, labeled container. Add a few drops of vinegar to each. What happens in each instance?

Which white powders can you identify by adding vinegar?

Conducting

Will some of the solids conduct electricity? Will their solutions conduct electricity?

Test the solids to see if they will conduct electricity (see Chapter 4, Experiment 13).

To a teaspoon of salt in a medicine cup, add an ounce of water. Will this solution conduct electricity? (See Chapter 4, Experiment 13). Do any other solids conduct electricity when mixed with water?

Which solids conduct electricity? Which solids dissolve in water to form conducting solutions?

Checking Your Science IQ

Ask an adult to prepare a mixture of two or three of the white powders you have been testing. Then see if you can identify the powders in the mixture by using the tests you have tried on all these solids.

Were you able to identify the powders that the adult gave you? How did you do it?

2. WHERE DOES THE GAS COME FROM?

Place one-half teaspoon each of starch, sugar, flour, baking soda, and salt in a cup. Add an ounce of water and stir. Drop an aspirin tablet into the mixture. What happens?

Which solid reacts with aspirin to produce the gas

you see forming bubbles in the mixture? Or do all the solids react?

On the basis of what you know about the solubility of these solids, their reactions with other chemicals, and the nature of aspirin in water (see Chapter 4, Experiment 2), see if you can predict which solids will react with aspirin in water to form a gas.

To test your prediction, add a piece of an aspirin tablet to a small sample of each solid in separate medicine cups or vials. Add a little water to each cup and look for the bubbles of gas you saw before. Which solids react with aspirin to produce a gas?

Did you predict correctly?

3. WHAT PUTS THE FIZZ IN ALKA-SELTZER®?

Read the label on an Alka-Seltzer® package. What chemicals are found in an Alka-Seltzer® tablet?

Some of these chemicals can be found in your kitchen (sodium bicarbonate is baking soda) or bathroom (aspirin). The others can be found in a school laboratory, chemistry set, pharmacy, or science supply house.

When you have gathered all the ingredients of Alka-Seltzer®, see if you can determine which chemicals are needed to produce the "fizz-fizz" when the tablets are dropped into water.

What gas do you think is produced when Alka-Seltzer® reacts with water?

How could you collect and test the gas to see if you are right?

4. Speedy and Not-so-Speedy Alka-Seltzer®

When you drop an Alka-Seltzer® tablet into water, it reacts to produce bubbles of carbon dioxide and a soluble salt.

Will the temperature of the water affect the rate at which Alka-Seltzer® produces carbon dioxide? To find out, place 4 ounces of hot water in one glass. Place 4 ounces of cold water in a second glass. Drop an Alka-Seltzer® tablet into each glass. Does the speed of this reaction depend on temperature?

Does the amount of surface area of the tablet affect the speed of the reaction? You can find out by crushing a tablet into tiny pieces. Add this crushed tablet and a whole tablet to separate glasses of water at the same time. Why should the amount and temperature of the water in the two glasses be the same? Which tablet reacts faster? Why do you think one tablet reacts faster than the other?

To see if the amount of water affects the speed of the reaction, add a tablet to a full glass of water. At the same time, add an identical tablet to a glass that is one-quarter full of water at the same temperature as that in the full glass. In which glass is the reaction finished first? Does the amount of water affect the speed of this reaction?

Will the speed of the reaction increase if you use more Alka-Seltzer®? Into one glass of water drop half a tablet. Into an identical glass of water, drop a whole tablet. Record the time, in seconds, for each reaction. Is the reaction faster in the glass with the whole tablet? Remember, if the reaction speeds were equal, half a tablet would take half as long to react as a whole tablet.

Drop a tablet into some water in which several other tablets have already reacted. This water contains dissolved carbon dioxide and other chemicals from the tablets you put in earlier. Do you think this tablet will react faster, more slowly, or at the same rate as a tablet dropped into an equal volume of fresh water? What do you find?

5. Cool Cells

As you have seen, chemicals react more slowly when they are cold. Changes that go on slowly inside a flashlight cell cause it to become "dead" after a time. For this reason, electrical cells are said to have a shelf life. They can only be kept on the shelf for a certain period of time and still be able to produce an electric current.

Perhaps the shelf life of flashlight cells can be made longer by keeping them cool. To find out, buy a few flashlight cells. Place about six of them in the refrigerator.

Put another six in one of your desk drawers. Every week or so test both sets of cells to see if they will still light a flashlight bulb.

What do you find the shelf life of flashlight cells to be? Do the cells that are kept cool have a longer shelf life? If they do, can you explain why?

6. ADDING BLACK TO MAKE CLEAR

You can buy some activated charcoal or carbon at a drugstore, a hobby shop, or a pet store. There may be some in your school that your teacher will give you. The carbon is often used to remove foul odors or colored impurities from water.

To see how activated carbon will react with other substances, add a drop of food coloring to each of two glasses of water. To one of the glasses add a small amount of activated charcoal and stir. The second glass will serve as a control. Cover both glasses with saucers and leave them overnight. What happens?

7. HARD AND SOFT WATER

Hard water has chemicals such as magnesium and calcium dissolved in it. Soft water contains very little of these chemicals. To see why people or cities that have hard water spend money to soften their water try this simple experiment.

Fill a test tube or a small jar about three-quarters full of hard water. (If you have no hard water, dissolve some calcium or magnesium sulfate in soft tap water.) To a second tube or jar add an equal amount of soft water. Put a drop or two of liquid soap in both water samples and shake their containers. What differences do you see?

8. WATCHING THE WEATHER

From your kitchen window you can watch the weather and keep a log of temperature, air pressure, humidity, wind speed, wind direction, rainfall, the amount of cloud cover, and the types of clouds. After you've kept weather records for a while, you'll find that you will be able to predict the weather better than most people. Just by paying attention to weather patterns such as changes in pressure, wind direction, temperature, and clouds, you'll begin to see that certain changes often precede a particular type of weather.

An indoor-outdoor thermometer that will measure maximum and minimum temperatures each day would be a handy instrument to have. You can measure air pressure with an aneroid barometer. You'll find that changes in pressure are often a good way to predict approaching fair or foul weather.

You can buy a combination rain gauge-wind speed meter for relatively little cost. And you can build a simple weather vane that will indicate wind direction.

A wet and dry bulb thermometer can be used to measure relative humidity or you can find the dew point* to determine both the relative and absolute humidity.

Now that you have learned some of the careful techniques used by scientists, you can go on experimenting, observing, and interpreting the results of your own experiments.

* Chapter 5 of *Science in Your Backyard,* by Robert Gardner and David Webster, Julian Messner, 1987, has useful information on setting up your own weather station. It will also explain how to measure dew points.

INDEX

125

INDEX

Index

ABOUT THE
AUTHOR

ROBERT GARDNER is head of the science department at Salisbury School, Salisbury, Connecticut, where he has taught biology, energy, physics, chemistry, and physical science. He did his undergraduate work at Wesleyan University and has graduate degrees from Trinity College and Wesleyan University. He has taught at a number of teachers' institutes and is the author of many books for young readers, including *Water, The Life Sustaining Resource, The Whale Watchers' Guide, Science Around the House, The Young Athlete's Manual*, and, with David Webster, *Science in Your Backyard*.